After Survival

After Survival

ONE MAN'S MISSION IN THE CAUSE OF MEMORY

Leon Zelman

with Armin Thurnher

Translated from the German by

Meredith Schneeweiss

HOLMES & MEIER

New York / London

Published in the United States of America 1998 by
Holmes & Meier Publishers, Inc.
160 Broadway   New York, NY 10038

Copyright ©1998 by Holmes & Meier Publishers, Inc.
Originally published in different form under the title *Ein Leben nach dem
Überleben*, copyright © 1995 by Verlag Kremayr & Scheriau, Vienna.

Grateful acknowledgment to the Austrian Cultural Institute
which provided support for the publication of this book.

Typesetting by Coghill Book Typesetting.
This book has been printed on acid-free paper.

Library of Congress Cataloging-in-Publication Data

Zelman, Leon, 1928–
    [Leben nach dem Überleben.   English]
    After survival : one man's mission in the cause of memory / Leon
Zelman with Armin Thurnher : translated from the German by Meredith
Schneeweiss.
      p.   cm.
    ISBN 0-8419-1382-X (alk. paper)
    1. Zelman, Leon, 1928– . 2. Jews—Poland—
Biography. 3. Jewish
    children in the Holocaust—Poland—Łódź—Biography. 4. Holocaust
    survivors—Austria—Vienna—Biography. I. Thurnher, Armin, 1949–
. II. Title.
    DS135.P63Z3913   1998
    940.53'18'092—dc21
    [B]   97-49957
                                                            CIP

Manufactured in the United States of America

For all mothers

CONTENTS

Preface   ix

CHAPTER ONE
My Shtetl Szczekociny   *1*

CHAPTER TWO
In the Lodz Ghetto   *23*

CHAPTER THREE
Surviving Auschwitz   *57*

CHAPTER FOUR
A Displaced Person   *85*

CHAPTER FIVE
Making Vienna Home   *129*

Epilogue   *163*

PREFACE

I don't want to write a book about the Holocaust. So much has already been described, analyzed, put into figures about the Holocaust that my recollections add but one more testimony to the best-documented event in history. I want to tell a story that leads through the horror of the Holocaust to the present day—my story.

I want to write a book about the Jewish mothers and fathers, the girls and boys of my shtetl at a time when my contemporaries and I began to dream. As a child I could have imagined almost anything, but never what actually happened. Today it seems to me that I lived in an environment that was conducive to dreaming big dreams. Yet before everyday life could bring these dreams down to earth, which is what one would expect, the community of dreamers was torn apart and destroyed, and the dreamers themselves were annihilated.

The bud of our youth had barely begun to open when it was crushed. Much later, when I was honored for my life achievements I said, "You see before you one of the few survivors of a lost generation that perished in concentration camps, in forests, in ghettos, and on death marches. I want to tell about what kind of a generation that was."

I want to talk about that generation and about what perished with it. Beyond our physical annihilation, the Nazis tried to dehumanize us, to strip us of everything human. They wanted to bring us to the point that when a father died we thought only about taking his bread; that when a friend collapsed, the first thing we tried to do was to take his shoes. They wanted us to steal, lie, and betray, going to any lengths to stay alive.

What Hitler wanted was to destroy the strength and the self-respect of an entire generation of Jews. The "master race," the SS, sought to turn us into subhuman creatures, into "human animals." I want to show, not only for myself, but for all those who shared my fate, that he did not succeed.

When I told my friends that I was planning to tell the story of my life, I could feel their support. Like them, I am one who survived the camps as a child and escaped the destruction that was intended for us all.

I chose a career in journalism and a lifelong commitment to serving the Jewish community in large part to carry out my moral struggle against Hitler. I am pleased that my friends are proud of me, and I have written this book for them as well as myself.

Let me return to the beginning of my story—to the Polish shtetl where I was born in 1928.

CHAPTER ONE

My Shtetl Szczekociny

I never went back. For a long time I tried not to remember, although I knew that its image would always be with me. Now when I try to remember, the first thing that comes to mind is a gentle, nostalgic song that my mother used to sing to me: "Mayn Shteteleh Belz." It was an evening song, composed for a popular Yiddish film. The idealized shtetl of the song probably never existed, but it captures certain rhythms of life that I recall and my longings for a sweetness that is no more.

Our shtetl has been extinguished; it perished—destroyed, burned, and wiped out together with the traces of my relatives who died in the Nazis' storm of destruction. Yet they should not be forgotten, and small-town Jewish life should not be forgotten.

Szczekociny, which was the name of our shtetl, was situated between the cities of Zawiercie and Kielce in Silesia, a province in western Poland. The population was mostly made up of Jews. Merchants, crafts-people, shoemakers, tailors and blacksmiths lived in a community together, with God and the Torah, His Law. We lived in this small, close community, without imagining that anything could be different.

It seemed to us that time flowed by as smoothly as the Pilica, the river that separated the city into two parts.

On one side of the Pilica lived the Jews; on the other there was a mixed population and a large church. The Jews had two synagogues. Jews and Christians lived side by side in mutual tolerance. The events of the year passed in peaceful succession, and one year was like the next. Once there was a fire that destroyed half of the city. This event, it was thought, would give whole generations something to talk about.

Religious life determined the course of daily events. The week seemed to be divided into the days preceding and the days following the Holy Sabbath, which was the pinnacle of the week: a day of services, rest, and joy. It was to give Jews a "taste of paradise" on earth. Wednesday, in contrast, was the busy market day, when all endeavors were focused on business.

Prior to the Sabbath all efforts went into preparation for the holiday. After the sun went down on Friday, the start of *erev shabbes* (Sabbath eve), no more work could be done until the end of the Sabbath. So all day Friday the women hastened to finish the shopping, bake the *challah*, prepare the festive meals, clean the house, bathe the children, and ready the festive clothes for everyone.

In the late afternoon the *shammes* would summon the men and boys to the *mikvah*, the ritual bath. Afterward the men went to the synagogue, while the women, already dressed in their best clothes, lit the Sabbath candles at home and waited for the return of the men, who would probably bring a guest along.

On Saturday morning the entire family went to the synagogue to take part in the services. Sometimes large or small groups went outside to talk in front of the synagogue. After lunch at home, quiet prevailed. Father and Mother went to sleep, everyone took a nap or a walk or otherwise spent the day at leisure. The marketplace seemed deserted.

When the third star appeared in the evening, Mother said the following prayer:

> God of Abraham, Isaac, and Jacob,
>   the holy Sabbath is nearing an end.
> May the new week bring us
>   health, life, and all that is good.
> May it bring us sustenance, good tidings,
>   deliverance and consolation.
> Amen.

Father extinguished the *havdalah* candle in wine. We wished each other a good week, as we did every week and went to bed.

Not only the course of the days but the course of the years in the shtetl were marked by religious observance. The majority of the Jews were Orthodox. Weddings, births, and deaths, good fortune and misfortune were acknowledged with traditional prayers and rituals.

Religious values also played a role in determining social status in the shtetl. Learning was a *mitzvah*, an act commanded by God. The commandment "to teach [the laws] diligently to one's children, to speak of them at home and on one's way, before lying down and upon rising," was reiterated daily in the *shema* and regarded as one of the most important of all 613 laws. Accordingly the rabbis and scholars were highly regarded. They were called the *sheyneh yidn*, "fine" or educated Jews, while at the other end of the social scale were the *prosteh yidn*, "common" or "coarse" Jews, meaning the uneducated who made their living as unskilled laborers, such as porters and water carriers. Since scholarship was prized, one could be a *sheyner yid* without being rich. Between the two extremes there was the broad middle class, to which my parents belonged. The shopkeepers and craftsmen, whose activities were at the heart of the shtetl's economy, were neither high nor low in class.

All Jewish boys in the shtetl went to *cheder*, the religious pre-school, where at three one began learning to read the prayers and *humash*, the five books of Moses. The sons of more religious Jews continued in *cheder* and went on to *yeshivah*. I went to the Polish elementary school after my early years in *cheder*.

The dictates of religious life were not as all-encompassing as they had been in the centuries before. Some families tried to emancipate themselves slightly from these constraints. Yet there was no question of assimilation, and indeed, assimilate to what? All Jews essentially observed the religious laws, the synagogue was full on holidays, and money was not touched on the Sabbath.

At the center of the shtetl was the counterpoint of religious life, the main square and marketplace, the center of all important events and of communications. Here the goal was to buy and sell, to exchange money and goods. Almost all the businesses and taverns surrounding the square were Jewish, with the exception of Kaletta, the large, imposing restaurant. The Jews didn't usually go there because it wasn't kosher. When they had something to celebrate, a circumcision, a wedding, or some other religious occasion, they preferred their own establishments.

Radio had just been introduced, but it was more a toy than a means of communication. When my parents gave me a primitive crystal receiver as a gift I took it proudly to school to show it off. The headphones went on—and you could hear music! Soon even Kaletta's in the marketplace had a radio with a loudspeaker that was mounted over the counter and blared out the door.

All kinds of sounds mingled with the noise of the marketplace—the market calls, the rolling wheels of horse-drawn wagons, the blacksmith's hammering, the murmuring of the central fountain, the conversations between farmers and shopkeepers.

Everyday life took place on the streets. Most of the unpaved streets led to dead-ends. Many houses were old, some were roofed with straw, some seemed to be falling apart. The craftsmen sat in their simple stalls crowded around the marketplace. With their white beards and long hair, they were imposing and at the same time often ragged figures.

The shopkeepers and craftsmen led their lives as if ordained by God. They did not serve scholarship, but spent their lives in the toilsome struggle for a meager living. Most of them were very poor. Saturday was their special day. On this day they allowed themselves the very best, as little as that may have been. No one went without his festive meal or refrained from dressing in his best. Indeed, if there was any way one could afford it, no one denied himself the charitable custom of inviting someone even more needy than himself to a Sabbath meal. The Christians respected the Sabbath, because on that day all the Jewish shops were closed. The Jews in turn respected Sundays.

The children passed by the large Christian church with a mixture of awe and curiosity; it was an ornate baroque structure, with a palace behind it. The people who went in and out of it were very rich, we told ourselves, and marveled.

Szczekociny was not a village but a small town. Five thousand people lived in the shtetl and most of them were Jews. It was a closed world resting within itself, which consciously denied itself more than the necessary contact with the outside world. And yet the outside world broke in.

The doors of Kaletta, the tavern at the market, were always open, and from outside one could see the people standing at the bar. Radio programs blew an aura of world politics out the open tavern doors onto the marketplace of the shtetl. Now and then the broadcast of a Hitler speech would drone over the square; I hardly understood what he was saying, but I was frightened by the threatening tone.

When Marshal Pilsudski died in 1935, the end of an era could be foreseen for many Jews. However nationalistically and dictatorially the autocrat Pilsudski may have governed Poland, the Jews had accepted him as a kind of protector. The large cities offered a cultural life in which the Jews could participate to a certain extent; emancipation and tolerance seemed possible. This changed with Pilsudski's successors; for instance, ritual slaughter of kosher meat suddenly became a topic for public discussion.

A member of the Sejm, the Polish parliament, introduced a law against ritual slaughter. This news was met with alarm at the marketplace in Szczekociny. I was eleven years old and up to that time I didn't know what anti-Semitism meant. Now I heard the word for the first time. Later it was obvious to me that anti-Semitism must have been a major topic, because the newspapers were full of it. Yet anti-Semitism did not factor very deeply in my childhood memories.

Like most Jewish boys my brother and I went to the local school and considered ourselves Polish. We couldn't and wouldn't imagine anything else. There were two schools, the Jewish one and the Polish one. The wealthier families sent their children to the Polish school because it was a better school, and taught the children Hebrew on the side. I myself did not learn Hebrew.

In the morning we went into the school yard and sang the Polish anthem: "May God protect Poland with all His might!" Even the Zionists sang Polish songs. The school consisted of three to four classes. The teachers liked me because I was good at reciting poetry—in Polish. When I came home Friday afternoons, I would lie on a soft rug on the floor and read the Polish author Henryk Sienkiewicz, as well as translations of Jules Verne and Karl May.

This pleased my mother. Even though these weren't religious texts, reading contributed to scholarship. My cousin had a whole bed full of books—he literally slept beneath books! I saw that when I visited him in Zawiercie. Szczekociny had a public library as well as the lending library at school. There was a lively exchange of books among the children. When someone went to Katowice, Warsaw, or Cracow he would bring back books. From Paris there was a French book or two. The girls collected illustrated magazines from Paris and Berlin, which were things we couldn't get at home. We turned the pages flushed with excitement at the scenes of unimagined elegance and fashion. The Schwarzbaum sisters and their friend Hanka Rinsky, just twelve years old, put on airs like ladies in high society, just because they possessed magazines like these. We craved anything in print that would tell us about life beyond our shtetl.

I remember we called one of our classmates Trotsky because of his looks. He was very intelligent, naturally a leftist. So you see, we knew of Leon Trotsky, the great Jewish revolutionary! It was something to be proud of, regardless of what one thought of his ideas. And the fact that there were Jewish parliamentarians in Warsaw was also something that made our chests swell with pride. Like typical boys we liked to talk about war, which was a big thing to us. Poland would win gloriously. We assured ourselves that the mounted Polish *uhlans* with their lances would be in Berlin in one to two days if the Germans challenged them.

The public life of the city took place around the fountain at the marketplace. Here there was also an equestrian statue of General Kosciuszko. He was a Polish national hero who took part in the American War for Independence as an aide-de-camp to Washington and later fought against the Prussians as they approached Warsaw. Yet for us, the young Jews, there was a particular reason to admire him: a Jewish colonel named Berek Joselewicz had fought at his side. It was he whom we honored when we looked at Kosciuszko's statue.

Naturally, most of our market chatter didn't consist of honoring heroes, but of gossiping. We discussed who had come for a visit, who was in love with whom, and other small-town news. At the marketplace one met students who were home on vacation. There was no university in Szczekociny. Thus the children of the wealthy had to go to the big cities to study, to Lodz, to Warsaw, many also went to Vienna, some even to Paris. On warm summer evenings they would tell us all about the big world outside Szczekociny.

Their excursions into the wide world were not always completely voluntary, but rather because there was a *numerus clausus* for Jews at Polish universities. The sons of the Englander, Greipner and Borenstein families, who went to Paris to study, were the pride of the shtetl. But they had to go to Paris because they couldn't find a place to study in Warsaw, not because they weren't qualified, but because they were Jews. That was something one didn't like to mention. A son or daughter studied in Paris, that was great. Why talk about the fact that he had been turned down in Warsaw?

The marketplace was spacious and rectangular. All the most important shops on the square belonged to Jews; our grocery store was also there. We had a monopoly on sugar and salt and also sold petroleum. There was even a service station in the shtetl. There were buses, and now and then someone came in a private car. That would always cause a sensation, and a crowd of children would run after it. The car's occupants wore knickerbockers, aviator goggles, and leather caps and seemed very conscious of their own importance.

For me, Mondschein the blacksmith was at least as exciting as the cars and their passengers. I could watch the small, powerful man with his leather apron for hours—how he made the iron glow in the hearth, how he quieted down the uneasy horses by stroking them, how he trimmed their hooves and put on fresh shoes. His smithy was by the river. I always wondered how he could get the iron so hot in his fire that he could shape it with his hammer.

The shoemaker was named Silberstein. I also liked to watch him at work, especially when he hand-sewed shoes just for me. He also owned a small manufacturing business, where shoes were made by machine, and a shop at the marketplace where he sold them. But Silberstein's hand-sewn shoes were something special. Some of these craftsmen were philosophers, and although they didn't want to change the world, they could talk for hours about the course of events.

My family, as I said, was neither rich nor poor; there weren't any really rich people in Szczekociny. Our parents gave gifts of clothes to the children of the poor at the holidays, because then everyone was supposed to be well dressed. Everyone did his best to have a well-laid table on Friday night and if possible to invite a poorer member of the community, a *yeshivah* student or an itinerant peddler to dinner. Everyone knew that there were still poorer people whom one felt obliged to help. On Friday evenings these poor stood in little groups in front of the synagogue or study house and anyone who could, took one person or a whole family home to dinner. They related where they came from and what they had seen and experienced on their travels. In this way we learned about each other and enriched each other by exchanging information.

Around Szczekociny lay smaller villages whose inhabitants came to our town to trade their agricultural products for tools, clothing, hats and the like. Jews and Christian farmers met one another at the market and traded goods. In this way they got to know one another and kept each other abreast of what was going on.

Every Wednesday, on market day, horse-drawn wagons came from all over. Farmers sold their goods, brought their animals—chickens, rabbits and goats. With their earnings they bought goods from the shtetl and frequented the Jewish taverns.

The world of our shtetl was hardly as homogenous as it might appear from outside. One heard about new ideas at the fountain or in the small, elegant restaurant Sonnenschein, where the worldly-wise youth met. And we had radio and newspapers. The Jews didn't go to the Christian-owned tavern and at Sonnenschein one didn't have to deal with drunks. For the children the main attraction on the square was Lentschner, the big coffeehouse on the corner of the market. They had the finest cakes, and with the coins we had saved we bought a lollipop or a bit of chocolate there on the way home from school.

Of course I was too small to go to Sonnenschein's, but I went by often and saw the twenty-year-olds conversing. Sometimes I even went in, to buy myself a sandwich—the food there was very good. How I envied the older boys, who could invite girls to eat with them there!

The atmosphere there was full of ideals, although not all of the boys knew exactly what they wanted to do differently. They didn't want to break up the old world or have any hostile confrontations with it, but they wanted to break out of it. They exchanged books and information and stimulated each other with ideas. The air was charged with the exuberance of youth, with its infatuations and little affairs.

Often the talk concerned the ideas of Theodor Herzl, who had founded a movement called Zionism. It was a concept that was in complete contradiction to the world of the shtetl. "We are seeking our redemption in this world," cried the Zionists, and tackled the task in practical terms.

Small groups of people were formed called *challutzim*. These were young people who were not willing to leave their fate to God's intervention. They were Zionist pioneers who felt responsible for their own fate and who were preparing to emigrate to the land of Israel. Some families sent their children to Palestine. When they returned they told of the difficulties of being a pioneer, of the harshness of daily life there. This didn't stop the *challutzim* from dreaming of this country; it inspired them even more.

We listened to their talk with flushed cheeks. Another group, the young socialists, discussed socialism—a world full of equality and brotherhood. Of course the picture of socialism they invoked had a romantic tinge; these young people didn't know anything about the reality of Communism or Stalin. The sheltered sons of wealthy families took it as one of the privileges of youth to belong to these groups, to envision utopias, to take part in perspectives that would shape the future.

The majority were socialists. They accused the older ones of not doing anything about the future. Some of the young people no longer went to the synagogue but most of them did, out of respect for their parents and grandparents. One Sabbath, to disturb the service and get attention, some young socialists threw a white dove into the synagogue. The rabbis were outraged. "A *chutzpah!* A *chutzpah!*" they yelled into the yard. The young socialists, who were nothing more than teenaged troublemakers, laughed into their sleeves.

The grandfather of these rascals would have slapped their faces, if they could have been caught, and the rebels would have had to take it, because no matter how provocative and rebellious things became in the shtetl, respect and esteem for the elderly was paramount.

Harmless tricks and teasing took place often enough. For instance, there was excellent ham in Kaletta's tavern. What fun it was to try these forbidden dishes in public, on the Sabbath, no less, and enrage our elders. But in spite of the wish for confrontation, the conflict between the generations remained far from a radical break. Although the young people wanted to change the world, for the most part they didn't want to hurt their elders.

This tentative groping toward a new world came into the old world like light comes through closed blinds. "God bless you," said the elders to a youth who was leaving for Paris, Palestine, or Vienna. What they meant was: "Will we ever see you again in our little shtetl, or will you forget us and our ways?"

Change and a desire for continuity lay side by side in Szczekociny. In the big cities like Zawiercie and Lodz the turmoil of the new era could be felt more strongly; tradition was much weaker. Regardless of which social utopia one felt drawn to, regardless of which social class one belonged to, in the shtetl, Friday evening had to be beautiful. Even if one had no money, the meal had to be a feast. It was impossible to imagine it without chicken or fish.

People did not have much time during the week. Nor did they place great importance on taking meals together. Everyone ate and drank when time allowed. But on the Sabbath we took time for each other, on the Sabbath tranquillity reigned, conveying to all of us a feeling of belonging together: old and young, *rebbe* and *challutzim*, the water carrier and socialist student.

On the Jewish holidays the children played and danced on the square in front of the synagogue. But I was different—I always wanted to listen when the grown-ups were talking. (These "grown-ups" were two or three years older than I.) They argued with the elders. I would hear some words I didn't understand. They talked about anti-Semitism or what was going to happen to Poland. The elders had only one answer: trust in God. That was not enough for the young people.

There was a beautiful forest close to the shtetl. On Saturdays and Sundays the *challutzim* as well as the socialists went to these woods. The one group, to practice sports, sing Hebrew songs, to prepare themselves for Palestine according to Herzl's ideas; the others, to create a kingdom of justice on earth. The best of our youth met there. They were all curious about what was new, wanted to hear and learn about new things, wanted to develop and educate themselves. They respected the old world but did not accept it. These youths did not bicycle to the woods on the Sabbath to hear debates about socialism and Zionism. They did not ride until Sunday, when even the rabbi could not have anything against riding bicycles.

The generation that went to the woods no longer went to religious schools. It was a generation in transition. They were not conscious of the fact that a hundred years earlier Jewish youths like themselves went into the woods to read Schiller in secret. In its time even *Haskalah*, the Jewish enlightenment, had to be smuggled out of the woods into the shtetl.

The young people no longer discussed things in front of the synagogue, where they couldn't or didn't want to argue with the elders. These youths rebelled against the fatalism of their parents and grandparents, against their deep, unconditional belief in God. Perhaps they also felt the danger of becoming defenseless through this passivity. The young people left, when they could, for Russia, or they emigrated to Palestine. The elders, who could not leave, remained fatalists, entrusting their fate to God.

Of my grandparents I loved one grandmother especially. Of all our relatives—over four hundred of them lived in our shtetl alone—she was my favorite. The road that led to my grandmother's house was not paved. We usually visited her on the Sabbath. I admit that I was a bit in awe of her, perhaps because she was so tall and stately. Nevertheless, it was a great treat to visit her. There were always delicious baked goods at Grandmother's, and always a lot of company. We children liked to play with the chickens, geese, and goats in her yard.

The women were the strength of the shtetl society, in many ways stronger than the men. They lived a practical life that a child could observe and understand. Fathers worked to earn a living, and studied to get closer to God. The women were closer to the children. We lived with them and through them. When my mother got ready for the Sabbath, when she put the Sabbath bread into the oven, when she lit the candles and sang her melancholy songs, when she fought for the best price for a fish at the market, when she bandaged me after I fell off my bicycle and spanked me at the same time, because she worried when I rode my bicycle, all this I could understand. At such times she was close to me.

My little brother Shayek and I were always with our mother. Our father remained a distant figure, particularly when he immersed himself in his religious duties—when he went to the *mikvah* with a stern expression on his face, when he intoned the Hebrew ritual prologue at the Sabbath meal in words that I didn't understand, or went to the synagogue to study with the other men. Even when he questioned me on the Sabbath, to inquire about the progress of my studies, he seemed remote and strange to me. I observed his deeds, but I did not experience them intimately as I did my mother.

I remember other relatives of mine more vividly. My young cousin Idka was a seamstress; she was beautiful and I greatly admired her because she already went out with boys. She moved to Lodz in 1937 with her mother, Aunt Mejci and her family. I was to see her there later, under much less happy circumstances.

Mother thought that it wouldn't hurt me to spend some time with a religious family. Four times a year she sent me to Zawiercie, where one of her sisters, my aunt Ruchele, lived. Her husband, Yankel, was a

glass craftsman, but he was also a scholar, a learned man, and a philoso-
pher, such as could often be found among Jewish craftsmen. He was of
small stature and had an extremely well-groomed beard. He always
dressed in shabby but clean clothes, and had a strange way of looking
at material things. When passing shops with him or going through the
marketplace, it seemed as though the things that attracted me did not
even exist for him. His appearance and behavior proved him to be not
only a religious Jew but a wise one as well.

Uncle Yankel took me by the hand and led me to the synagogue not
only to pray, but also to explain many religious ideas to me. Although he
was a simple craftsman and my father was only a shopkeeper, they hoped
that their sons would rise above their class and for that they needed
knowledge.

I profoundly respected this scholarly glass-worker. Despite all of my
curiosity about the world, my inner alienation from traditional Judaism,
and a slight feeling of boredom mixed with reverence, I willingly accompanied Uncle Yankel to the synagogue to hear the holy Torah.

I looked forward to my trips to Zawiercie, to having new people to
talk to and seeing a new city. I also looked forward to Aunt Ruchele's
famous baked dumplings. (She was, by the way, not only an excellent
cook, but also beautiful to look at.) These dumplings more than repaid
me for the toil of my religious-philosophical instruction.

Of her two sons, Usher, the older one, was a socialist. He gave
high-minded speeches using many words that were unknown to me. The
younger one, Shmulek, was quiet, a Zionist dreamer who read a lot
about Palestine. Their sister Hanka was my age. Of our four hundred
relatives in approximately 80 families in Szczekociny, she was one of the
few who survived, and she and her husband Jack are like brother and
sister to me today. Hanka was my only point of reference to my family
history and one of my most important sources.

Once a family photo of all the relatives was being taken. The event
turned into a family celebration in the Pilica field. Placing everyone to

the photographer's satisfaction seemed to take forever. Then he disappeared under his cloth and frightened us with a puff of smoke. That photo is lost like everything else. I only know we stood in the grass in front of the bushes, and that I stood in bare feet grinning into the camera.

Due to the high value placed on scholarship in the shtetl, illiteracy hardly existed among the Jews. There were almost no Jews who couldn't read (at least Yiddish or Hebrew), in contrast to the illiteracy of the local peasant population. For this reason, new ideas were more easily available to the Jews than to the surrounding population. And weren't we all looking for salvation? Who said that it could be found only in the synagogue and not in the Soviet Union or in Palestine?

But these ideas were no more than cautious conjectures, at most they were a slight ripple in the peaceful stream of a traditional life. "Leon," friends later said to me, "they were all poor people in the shtetl, but they were all happy to be Jews." They loved living together, the security of this self-contained world with its peaceful Sabbath and its pre-Sabbath excitement. This life, in its modest way, holy through and through, was supported by caring mothers like mine and Aunt Ruchele and by serious fathers like mine and my Uncle Yankel, the glass-worker. And somehow, even the young rascals were a part of it.

Life kept its holiness even after modern times had begun to permeate the shtetl, as when one of the first buses began its route between Szczekociny and Zawiercie. We no longer had to travel by the slow bumping horse-drawn wagons and slow, rocking trains—which took a whole day—to visit Aunt Ruchele. In fact, it was my cousin Silberstein who made money with his idea of a bus line. The new buildings constructed after the fire in the shtetl gave witness to the new era. But most of all, the way was paved for the new era by sending the children to schools outside the shtetl.

I was a clever child and listened to all the talk: of the young, snobbish students home from abroad and of the old, devout Jews who trusted in God for everything. I listened, too, to the conversations of young lovers; I did not really know what they were talking about, although a sweet longing came over me just the same. I listened to the excited political disputes of the young people; they spoke about books of which I, naturally, didn't understand a thing. I was gripped by a longing to expand my horizon, to grow up, to travel; a longing for life and love. This longing for more, for things beyond the shtetl colored my whole childhood.

I had a large circle of friends, among them many non-Jews. I found them interesting mainly because they did not belong to our world. My girlfriend was called Basia. I idealized this little Christian girl so much because she seemed like the girl in Sienkiewicz's "Desert and Thornbush," which I was reading at the time. Everyone in the shtetl knew that we were in love and laughed about us, although the two of us thought we had a secret.

The young Jews did not feel that the shtetl was a ghetto. We felt no differences between Jews and Christians, except on market day, when perhaps a farmer who always mistrusted Jews felt he had been overcharged. But that kind of thing could also happen among Christians or among Jews. We did not feel that we were discriminated against; on the contrary, some of us viewed the Christians with pity because they did not have the Sabbath and thus had no knowledge of its blessings.

In school we associated widely with Polish Christians. I had my girlfriend, we wrote letters to each other, whispered together, and once we even kissed. That was strange for both of us, not because I was a Jew and she a Christian, but because children just feel funny when they kiss. She was blond and had blue eyes. I never saw her again. The entire family was shot by the Germans right after they invaded Poland.

Of course, I had Jewish girlfriends too. One of them was an especially sweet girl whose parents tended a *mikvah*. I can't remember her name, but I will never forget the strange scenes I witnessed when I visited her. I was led to the bath by her brother, who looked like a fifty-year-old, but was only twenty-five. The naked men were a shock for me—the hanging bellies, the pale bodies in the steam and the wan light. It was ghostly. I only endured it for the sake of this girl. It was obvious she wouldn't stay there very much longer; she wanted to get away from this environment.

Nadja Münz was the name of another girl, an especially pretty one, who came for the summer from nearby Sosnowiec, a larger town. Later her brother reminded me that I always tried to get her to go to the circus with me. Although I didn't have any money, I borrowed it from her brother, which is why he remembers it. He is still alive today in Israel. Nadja did not survive. On our walks, my friends and I only wanted to talk to her about one thing—it must have gotten on her nerves—we constantly asked her what life was like in the big city.

Life did not consist just of going to school, reading, and being in love. I tore around the shtetl on my bicycle, racing up and down the steep paths, and it terrified my mother when I didn't come home on time. But other children also had bicycles, so my parents couldn't really make me do without one. I also had a pigeon-breeding project at home. For years I was known throughout Szczekociny as "Leon the Pigeon Breeder." In addition, I had a German shepherd named "Rex"—or rather, he had me, because I failed to exert any authority over him. I could frequently be seen running down the streets after him, begging him to come back to me.

I also had a leather ball with which we played soccer on Sundays, when our elders' talk began to bore us. On any other day playing soccer—except at school—was unthinkable. The Sabbath and Wednesday market day governed the week and filled up three days and four evenings. Other evenings were spent at home; one might make a short visit to someone or borrow a book. It wasn't easy to spontaneously arrange to meet friends, after all there was no telephone. But as a child among poor people there was something special about having a leather ball. It made me a popular figure among the children.

The winters were very cold. We went to the river to watch the men breaking the ice with ice picks; the blocks were brought to the ice cellar. Next to our house was a soda factory, where the ice blocks were stored. Ice-skating on the frozen Pilica was not completely safe; once a schoolmate drowned.

The nearby mill was a meeting place, and various celebrations were organized there. We congregated there on the afternoon of Rosh Hashanah for *tashlich,* when we symbolically cast our sins into the water in the form of bread crumbs.

There was a beautiful field beside the river where cattle grazed; sometimes visitors came from the surrounding towns and cities, and I got away whenever I could to roam around there and study the strangers. A fair was even set up there, with a carousel, swings, and shooting stands.

Once a circus came, and it impressed me as it does every child who sees the glittering world of animals and clowns for the first time. I couldn't sleep the whole night, I was so deeply impressed by the images of the leaping acrobats and the people who risked their lives under the big tent. When I was allowed to go to the cinema to see a silent movie, I was more touched by the sad music of the piano player than by the movie. The people on the screen moved so quickly that afterward I always felt dizzy. Sometimes wandering Jewish acting companies performed in the cinema. Traveling klezmer musicians played at weddings or on the street. Once an airplane landed on the other side of the Pilica, to pick up someone who was ill. We all ran to it, so as not to miss this unprecedented spectacle.

No one spoke about death or war. Although we lived for the day, death also existed. It was not hidden from us. When a schoolmate died, a Christian, we all paid our last respects to her and filed by her coffin. Yet this death was not terrifying—for us Jews, the strange, uncomfortable feeling was not in confronting death for the first time, but rather the Christian customs with which they dealt with it, especially the open casket.

We were drawn to the mill, which was a large, modern building. We could not get our fill of watching the water rush onto the millwheel. Often when evening had passed, all of a sudden we became conscious of the cemetery wall on the other side of the path. We grew afraid, and headed for home.

One of my grandfathers died when I was ten, but I was not allowed to see the corpse. The rabbi came and blessed him as he lay dying in bed. A doctor also appeared, but could not save him. Sadness hit me as the shops closed, which they always did when the funeral processions went by, and I cried a lot. He was carried through the streets to the cemetery, but I did not really understand what death meant. Grandmother calmed and comforted us.

Saturday evening when the Sabbath was over, my mother sang songs. Except for "Mayn Shteteleh Belz," I can't remember any of the words. They were only partly directed at us, partly they praised God and His blessings. They were nostalgic, and despite all the joy of the Sabbath day, full of a sadness from which I could not free myself. Only on Sunday morning could I shake off this melancholy feeling. I went out with the young socialists or with the young Zionists. The socialists talked about improving the world, and their intellectuality fascinated me. The *challutzim* were more like pioneers, adventurers. What was important to me was that they spoke of the world outside; or better yet, they promised us the world outside. That was where I wanted to go.

We did not have a concept of riches or fame, but we pasted together a dream album of a different, larger, more colorful world and illustrated it with beautiful scenes from magazines as well as decals and photographs. Turning the pages of this album, looking at the portraits and decals, was a memorable part of my childhood.

One of my favorite photographs showed me with my Uncle Senderowicz, a trade-union secretary in Lodz. They talked about my uncle in the shtetl, and said he wasn't religious, and that in Lodz he did not go to the synagogue. But when he came to Szczekociny, he had to go to the synagogue, for his sister's sake. He was very elegantly dressed. A relative from the city with white spats who gave tips everywhere—that was something to be proud of.

He stroked my hair, asked what I was reading and if he could see my books. My mother praised her sons, so that he would be impressed with us. A man of the world, but from a different world, a socialist: that was how we young Jews envisioned a life fit for a human being. Here was someone from the world we had dreamed about, where we could live in dignity as Jews. He fought for the poor and oppressed, because feudalism still was at large in Poland. But we did not mean only the poor: by the oppressed we meant the Jews.

It must have been about 1938 when well-read people like the Jewish teacher at school began to speak more frequently about Germany, although the talk did not turn immediately to the subject of war. Gradually there was news about the change in the situation, which quickly led to discussions about a coming war. Then, suddenly, there was talk of nothing else.

Speeches about Poland echoed across the market. In the early thirties the short-sighted Poles had spoken about attacking Germany, and now it wasn't much different. Germany had not experienced any decisive resistance, said Poland's Foreign Minister Beck. Poland will show the Germans what decisive resistance is. Echoes of these strong words resounded all the way to our school in Szczekociny.

Repeating Polish propaganda, I went home and announced that we didn't have to worry, the Polish army would be in Berlin in two days with its mounted cavalry. Besides, nearly all Poles were of the opinion that the guarantees made by England and France would offer sufficient protection from the Germans; in case of war, the whole world would be on Poland's side.

The building of trenches began. The children welcomed the change. Euphoria and chauvinism predominated. Yet our parents were concerned about Hitler's speeches, heard out of the open doors of Kaletta's. At home we had neither radio nor telephone, and my crystal receiver was basically a toy; it did not serve as a conveyor of news. We didn't understand these speeches, but their tone frightened us. But what was there to be afraid of? The uhlans and our allies would protect us. Proudly we watched the cavalry set off through our city to keep their promise.

Some of the more intelligent and educated people had correctly understood Hitler's speeches. They were afraid and prepared to flee. The choice of escape routes and destinations was limited. The socialists went to Russia, the small group of Zionists to Palestine. Others went wherever it was possible to get visas. The old people remained. "You go," they said to the younger ones. "We're staying here. God will protect us." There was nothing else for the young to do but to run away, and they ran—they ran for their lives. The arrival of change had come in a way completely different from what we ever could have imagined and it had acquired a completely different meaning.

One morning in September 1939 planes flew over the village. From the sky came the howl of dive bombers; the bombs fell whistling to the ground. Worst hit was the marketplace, much of the shtetl lay in ashes. Then came the sound of guns and artillery.

That was the end of my shtetl. Never again would my mother sing my song there, the song that would always remind me of my shtetl. Along with my mother's song, and my father's prayer and the candles on *erev shabbes*, a tradition of hundreds of years of Jewish life in Poland came to an abrupt end. The old people perished as did the young, including those who had been on the verge of creating a new world so full of hope and promise.

Those who did not flee, died. I myself never went back. I won't go back. One doesn't visit crushed dreams.

One cannot even begin to understand the tragedy of the Holocaust—the enormity of the tragedy—without understanding the world of the shtetl. The Nazis did not only destroy people; they destroyed an entire culture when they destroyed this shtetl and thousands like it throughout Eastern Europe. They robbed its youth of their chance to take part in modern society. They destroyed a world and its ethos.

In the eighties I organized an exhibition in Vienna as a monument to this shtetl. The subject of remembrance would not be famous personalities but rather the lost world of Jewish life in the shtetl.

The town of Szczekociny still stands. At least a town of the same name. It has nothing in common with my shtetl.

I wanted to get myself a travel guidebook, to call to mind some topographical features, so I called the cultural department of the Polish embassy.

"You know," said the embassy employee, "there was a beautiful synagogue there." I asked him to send me material about it. He sent me a guide which does not waste a single word on the synagogue; it does not even mention that Jews ever lived in Szczekociny. Hitler obliterated this community so completely that it became possible to bury its memory. Despite that, I want everyone to know that my shtetl did exist. That's why I am telling this story.

Not all of Szczekociny's Jews perished. Almost none of the Jews who were sent to ghettos and camps survived. Those who went to Russia escaped with their lives, even if they were deported to Siberia. Probably there are still a few dozen people who knew the shtetl as I did. But none of those who fled and thus survived the German raid live there today.

CHAPTER TWO

In the Lodz Ghetto

The cavalry returned with their uniforms torn to shreds and their lances broken. They carried their dead and wounded with them; badly beaten, they trudged through the shtetl, dragging along the remains of their proud equipment. Men and horses were left lying dead in the street. Coldly precise and unmercifully exact, the Germans followed closely behind the uhlans.

They left nothing to chance. They knew all about Szczekociny. Some time ago a stranger had appeared in the shtetl and had looked around, here and there. Then he disappeared. No one had thought much about it. When the Germans came, everything was suddenly clear. Their informer—because everyone saw him now for what he was—stood in the middle of the marketplace and showed the conquerors what could be found where. Through him they were already informed; they knew the location of the town hall, the synagogues and schools, where to find goods that were worth confiscating, and where Jews could be found.

The Germans marched quickly. They brought death. Szczekociny on the Pilica had strategic importance. Their artillery started firing at the shtetl. Fighter planes attacked. Confusion, panic, and chaos erupted everywhere.

Our house was hit. Father was killed in a volley of gunfire.

The wave of retreating cavalry passed through Szczekociny, one uhlan dragging the next, bandaged and bleeding. Mostly on foot and without their horses, our proud defenders dragged their damaged war equipment behind them, leaving us to fend for ourselves. At the sight of the lancers my mother had grasped the situation. If this was how Poland's hopes looked, we had to take care of ourselves. Father was no longer here to give advice. She decided to flee to Lodz—with me and my brother Shayek, who was two years younger—to the home of our Uncle Senderowicz, the elegant union man. He was supposed to have a large apartment there. We also hoped to find her sister, my Aunt Mejci, who had moved to Lodz two years earlier after the death of her husband.

To Lodz! To the big city, that I had yearned to see for so long—although under different circumstances. Because I had been such a good student, my uncle promised to bring me to the city to attend Gymnasium. But now we fled forever, not just for a semester. The most important things we wrapped up in a bundle. Some underwear and clothes, dishes, cutlery; the silver candlesticks, which no Jewish family would voluntarily leave behind, were dug out of the rubble. We took along only what we could carry. I stuck in one of my books, a Sienkiewicz novel, of course. The swiftness of the Germans left us no time to ponder the choice.

In complete contrast to this swiftness, our flight proceeded very haltingly. The streets were full of carts, horse-drawn wagons and hand-carts, ox wagons, and columns of fleeing civilians and soldiers. Every few minutes we were fired upon by a dive bomber. We succeeded in saving ourselves from the aircraft fire only by jumping into the ditch on the side of the road. Afterward, when we got up, there were always some dead on the ground. We had to leave them behind. The German army was coming closer and closer.

The news hurried after us. One terrible tale followed the next; each refugee had another to tell. (We only perceived the names of those who had been killed in passing.) We fled from this news. We heard that the Germans had forced all the old religious Jews who had remained behind into the synagogue and then set the locked synagogue on fire. All of them burned to death. Anyone who had somehow survived the inferno was shot. No one who stayed in Szczekociny even one day longer than we did survived. Now we knew even more clearly what we were fleeing from.

Mother decided to turn off of the main road. How she was able to find the way was a riddle to me. My brother and I trusted her unquestioningly, she was all we had. Nothing from this flight remains clearer in my mind than my fright at seeing the dead lying in pools of blood after each air raid. Those that lay there from the last attack no one seemed to care about. How different they looked from that Christian girl in the casket, who had seemed so strange to us back in the shtetl! The image of how she lay peacefully on the bier, wreathed and beautifully dressed so that we could bid her farewell, made it seem like a slight irregularity in the even fabric of our lives.

Now this fabric was torn. No greater difference could be imagined than that between that delicate figure of the girl and the dead that lined the path of our flight, with their bloated bellies, distorted faces and bulging, fly-covered eyes. Hers was the first corpse that I ever saw in my life. The sight of my dead grandfather had been kept from me. But now there were hundreds, thousands of dead. They filled the ditches to the left and right of the road. They frightened me much more than the reports about the events back in Szczekociny. Neither my brother nor I could believe that our father, our neighbors, teachers, rabbis, friends, and acquaintances were all dead, but we didn't have to imagine the dead that we saw before us. They took our breath away. Numbly we staggered forward, clinging to mother's hand.

Mother was silent. We didn't see the expression on her face, nor could we read her thoughts. She pressed our hands and spoke to us. "Get up, keep going." Firmly she urged us on. Around her neck she carried a small sack of gold coins to use for food or lodgings or to pay people for their services. Although people were ready to help us on our way, as a clever woman she preferred not to count on it. A gold piece was always an advantage when it came to finding something to eat or a place to stay.

Mother developed strengths that I never believed she had, although they didn't surprise me. She took charge of things with a steady hand, just as she had guided our family life. Now she led us through the unfamiliar countryside to Lodz. In her quiet, steadfast way and with the little pouch around her neck, she always got where she wanted to go. This consisted of finding someone to take us from one place to the next; usually these were farmers, once even Polish soldiers. After we left the main roads on which the Germans were marching, we fled through the woods and fields. Sometimes, when we saw German soldiers advancing down a road, we hid ourselves, because we knew they shot fleeing civilians whenever they felt like it.

We wandered along through a sunny Indian summer. Sometimes our path was covered with early morning fog, from which emerged villages and farms, with names I never heard of. People streamed towards Lodz from all directions. A strange autumn procession was taking shape, the beginning of a long trek. Despite the death and horror that were behind us, hardly anyone could imagine where it would lead.

Right now, Lodz was the safe haven that had to be reached. Everything would turn out all right in Lodz; we would be safe with our wealthy uncle. But we still had to go on through the villages.

Rooms were hard to find because so many refugees had the same goal: Lodz. Most of the time we were happy to be allowed to sleep in the hay in some barn. If a farmer gave us a bed, Mother would put my brother and me into it. She would cuddle up to us first, more to protect us with her body than to warm us. I felt for her breast like a small child, to feel her close to me. When we had fallen asleep, she crept out and lay on the floor so that we could sleep better.

Once in a larger village she was able to get a room. They must have been acquaintances, because Jews occupied the whole house. We were given a lovely room. Mother didn't have to sleep on the floor this time, as there was a chair. As always she left the bed to my younger brother and me. The room was furnished solidly and panelled with dark wood. The pendulum of a large grandfather clock swung back and forth. We had never seen such a clock before. It ticked loudly and struck every quarter hour with a mighty gong. This unfamiliar sound awakened and frightened us. Shayek started to cry. So Mother lay down next to him on the edge of the bed, took him in her arms and sang in a low voice, "Sleep, baby, sleep . . ." She sang it softly and sadly. She sang as though she knew everything that was to come. She sang it until my brother fell asleep.

In the middle of the night the clock awakened me again. I saw my mother praying. She was begging God for help. "What will become of us? Help us, Lord," I heard her murmur. I understood only part of her prayer, but it wasn't what she said that was so important. It was the plaintive, melancholy tone of that prayer and those songs that I knew from the shtetl, when we two boys were alone with her at home, waiting for Father to come home from the synagogue. Then Mother would light the candles and recite prayers, wishes and pleas for all her loved ones and relatives. She always cried a little, in weighing the extent of the misfortune that had to be averted.

In my sheltered youth, danger was never real to me. Danger was something that the ever-worried mothers used to talk about to keep their children from swimming in the river or being a dare-devil on their bikes. Only now, after Father's death, the loss of our home and all our possessions, being torn away from our roots, did I understand the sad tone of my mother's prayer. And only now that I understood it, did it touch my heart.

• • •

After four or five days we reached Lodz. Or was it two weeks? Today I can't estimate the time or the length of our route. I can't remember the detours we took and can't find the name of the places we went through on any map. On forest paths and by-ways, through unknown villages and countryside, we were led by this woman who had scarcely ever been out of a shtetl herself. After all, Szczekociny is about ninety miles from Lodz. Even today this feat is inconceivable to me. How did she get the idea of taking us to Lodz? How she found the right direction, bargained with farmers, found wagons that would take us, discovered short-cuts, and found food is incredible to me. Only when I think about it do I remember that I never saw her eating anything.

Finally in Lodz! The big city at last! Hordes of people, noise, tall buildings with thousands of windows, wide, magnificent boulevards, busy shops. Cars went by, streetcar bells rang. A large Julius Meinl store offering luxurious foods struck my eyes. How could this obvious urban normality be possible? The German occupiers had long since arrived here, flags with swastikas hung everywhere, Hitler Youth marched in white socks beside the cold elegance of the black SS uniforms. Where did they all come from? How could the Germans be here so quickly? Had there ever been a war?

True, in Lodz there had always been many ethnic Germans, most of whom went over immediately to the Nazis. On the other hand, over 200,000 of the 700,000 inhabitants of Lodz were Jews; the Jewish community of Lodz was among the world's largest and the head of the German district administration estimated that another 100,000 Jews had come to Lodz since the occupation.

Of course, only at first glance did everything appear as normal as it was supposed to be. Here and there you could see bomb rubble. Lodz had been attacked from the air. For the first time I heard someone calling me "Jew" in Polish. Although I was dressed like an ordinary schoolboy and one couldn't tell the difference between me and a Polish boy, the Poles knew exactly with whom they were dealing. They probably wanted to impress the Germans with their own anti-Semitism, which had a long and ugly tradition in Poland. Nevertheless, before I heard the German "*Jude*" I became acquainted with the Polish insult "*Zhid!*" in Lodz for the first time.

But worst of all, my uncle, to whom our path led us first, was not there. His wife opened the door to us with a pale, tear-stained face. Due to his leading position in the metal-workers union, her husband had been hung by the Germans with many other members of the Polish political intelligentsia at Baluty Square in Lodz's Old City. "First we had to get rid of the leaders of the Opposition . . . that was the political intelligentsia. They had to go and that was it." This statement by the head of the SS, Heinrich Himmler, explained the deadly plans behind the seemingly arbitrary brutality of the Germans. The fact that my uncle was a Jew had nothing to do with his execution. With this first step the Nazis wiped out any possible Polish resistance.

My uncle's widow—I should say "my aunt," but we didn't know her at all and Mother hardly knew her—took her situation with composure. Despite her shock and pain, she took us in and let us stay there for the time being. Although the horror was just beginning, everyone had already suffered some sorrow; no one could consider his loss to be an isolated case.

My aunt seemed to be a very educated and cultured lady; she helped us, strangers to the big city as we were, whenever she could. Yet we felt insecure in her elegant apartment. With our traditional religious background, we couldn't help her very much in her mourning for her atheist husband. And before we could get to know each other better, my aunt disappeared. Was she abducted? Arrested? We never found out.

Aunt Mejci took us in, and there we felt better. Her large family, three sons and three daughters, were like a part of the shtetl. We lived in a good middle-class quarter in a large house over a passage connecting Sienkiewicza with Piotrkowska, a heavily-trafficked boulevard. Beautiful ladies promenaded there, elegant cars stopped in front of expensive

restaurants. One could hear officers speaking German. I was overwhelmed. The flags, the drumming of the marchers, the stomping of
the boots on the pavement almost made me want to march along, too.
I couldn't get enough of the sounds of the streetcar: its ringing, the way
it screeched as it came to the next stop. These were the sounds of the
big new world I had dreamed of. The windows of the large stores provided the accompanying pictures. I stood round-eyed in front of them.

Things pass quickly for children. Despite all the terrifying experiences, despite the dead, despite the loss of my father and uncle, despite
the shock I had been subjected to since the beginning of our flight, I
was fascinated by the big city. Everything in Lodz seemed to be completely normal, with the exception of the swastika flags. In these first
weeks one still saw Jews on the streets, at least in our quarter, a "mixed"
or "better off" residential area. We heard that the Germans had been
harassing Orthodox Jews, but saw nothing of this ourselves. While now
and then a German might beat or harass someone for no apparent reason, it was not yet evident that the persecution of Jews was their primary objective.

Despite everything we had experienced, it wouldn't have occurred
to us that we were being persecuted as Jews. What was so special about
being a Jew? I, who felt like a Pole anyway, couldn't understand. It
wasn't until we heard the order that all Jews had to register that we
began to change our views. This order was followed by a nightly curfew.
When one paid a visit to someone else, one had to stay there for the
night. Even an eleven-year old could see that this was no longer part
of the routine of the big city, that something was wrong. Now even we
recognized the danger.

I began to grasp that I was being shut out. In the large courtyard,
where hundreds of families lived, I saw the Polish children running,
jumping, and playing soccer. It was forbidden for Jewish children to play
with them. How I would have loved to show the others how well we
could play soccer in Szczekociny! We were not allowed to enter Julius

Meinl's, the large store, something we had been looking forward to so much. As of November 14, there was an additional decree by the German administrator of Lodz, Friedrich Übelhör, requiring all Jews to wear a yellow armband, and as of December 13 to wear a yellow star with the word "Jew" on it. This had to be visible on the front and back. There were more frequent raids. Without giving any reasons, Jews were arrested, beaten, and dragged off for forced labor.

At the time we didn't say "the Nazis," we said "the Germans," *Ashkenaz*. The Jewish inhabitants of the thousands of shtetls in Poland were the descendants of German Jews, who had emigrated eastward from Germany hundreds of years ago. They called themselves *Ashkenazim* because they came from Germany. Now, thanks to a twist of fate, *Ashkenaz* and *Ashkenaz* stood face to face. The irony that the same word characterized both groups was lost on the persecutors and the persecuted.

Despite the registration, despite the armband and star, the Jews did not realize what was coming. Now and then one heard about a Jew who had killed himself out of desperation. Others left their possessions behind and fled to the east. Those remaining behind shook their heads. Why put oneself in danger? The hardships will ease up, somehow we'll make it through.

Our mother's face had not brightened since we left Szczekociny. It was not clear to her children—who couldn't understand why they were not allowed to play with the Polish children in the yard—what was happening. I wasn't even capable of making a connection between the Germans and the death of my father and uncle. We heard no political commentaries from my mother. She recognized the danger, but she kept her worries to herself. She packed them into her prayers, her melancholy songs and accompanying tears. Whatever was to come, she would protect us, fold us in her arms and make it through. They were still strong arms.

On the streets other Jews asked us children to help remove the rubble left from the bombing. There were notorious commandos that rounded up Jews and forced them for no reason to dig a ditch, only to give orders to fill it up again. At Christmastime 1939 enormous signs were put up saying that all Jews had to move into the ghetto. The ghetto was planned in an area of the Old City of Lodz, the area by the name of Marysin near the Jewish cemetery and the ill-reputed slum district around Baluty Square, where the public execution of my uncle and his fellow victims had taken place. The non-Jewish population of these areas had to move out and were given substitute apartments, of which there was now no shortage.

The winter of 1939–40 was terribly cold. Under the merciless eyes of the Germans in command, a large migration began in early February 1940. I didn't ask why we were moving again. How would explanations have helped? As many Jews did not voluntarily comply with the Nazis' demand to move into the ghetto, in March the SS stormed into the apartments of one district and caused a bloodbath. In panic after this "bloody Sunday" the Jews gathered up their belongings and fled to the ghetto. The final closure of the ghetto was not due until April 30, but already the alternatives were to follow orders or die immediately.

Measures that served to "protect the Jews" were willingly followed, because the consequences of not following them had been made sufficiently clear. The most cynical measure the Nazis employed was that only in rare cases would they dirty their own hands. They left this work to the victims—a principle that was also applied in the concentration camps: the worst henchmen were prisoners. They were personally responsible for seeing that orders were carried out. After all, it was that or their own lives.

In October 1939, following this principle, the Nazis had selected a Jewish ghetto administrator, even before the ghetto had been set up. Mordecai Chaim Rumkowski, former director of an orphanage, was given this task, probably due to his organizational skill. The ghetto— considered by the Nazis to be only a preliminary step to what they termed, in Hermann Göring's terrible words, "the Final Solution to the Jewish question"—was to function as a self-administered entity, cost as little as possible, and cause neither uproar nor unrest. In addition, it encompassed industrial enterprises and manufacturing facilities which had to be administered.

Thus the ghetto served to "protect the Jews." Rumkowski's concept was: "Our only way is work." As food could be obtained only from outside, from the Nazis, he based his plans on making the Nazis so dependent on the almost free delivery of goods from the ghetto, that in their own interest they could not liquidate the ghetto. It seems as though Rumkowski was actually able to delay the final liquidation of the ghetto by a year through the productivity of the ghetto's industrial enterprises.

The Nazis showed Rumkowski at the beginning of his administration who the real masters of the ghetto were when they instructed him to choose a Jewish Council with thirty-one members. Immediately after they were appointed they were deported by the Nazis. Rumkowski, who tried to prevent this, was brutally beaten up by the Gestapo and forced to appoint a new council.

In the Lodz ghetto Rumkowski lived like a king, lord over life and death. Outside the ghetto he was nothing, a puppet of the Gestapo. Inside the ghetto he even had stamps printed with his portrait. He was the head of the Jewish ghetto police, the courts and prisons, food and health administration, and the entire output of the ghetto. His administration had developed into a bureaucracy that comprised thirteen thousand people.

Even today, it is difficult for me to judge Rumkowski. He was a pawn of the Germans and in that role simply tried to save what could be saved. As the systematic extermination of the Jews commenced, he let himself be drawn increasingly into fulfilling the quotas of his bosses. His Jewish ghetto police assisted with deportations. He himself had announcements posted in which he urged mothers to give up their children and families, their old and sick. They were signed" "Ch. Rumkowski. Head of the Jews in Litzmannstadt." (On April 11, 1940, Lodz had been renamed "Litzmannstadt" by the Nazis.) As Rumkowski became more and more entangled in the Nazis' plans, he still stubbornly followed his own concept of saving what he could—the Jewish youth. I myself owe my life to him. My mother died in his ghetto.

How can one judge something like that? "Don't make a hero out of Rumkowski, even if you owe your life to him," I was admonished by one of my fellow sufferers who survived the ghetto. At his end, through the equalizing power of death, Rumkowski returned to the community of Jews that he had briefly left to become "King of the Jews."

Indeed, he ruled like a king and was called "King." The coach in which he rode through the ghetto was drawn by a gray horse. Later on, it was the only vehicle in the ghetto that was not drawn by human power. The King's coach was a striking contrast to the human-drawn excrement wagon or corpse wagon. It symbolized the privileges of the hated ghetto bigwigs who had enough to eat and the means to heat it, while the masses died of starvation.

No wonder that considerable political opposition formed against Rumkowski. But the strikes and protests collapsed after a few days because the strikers could not endure starvation. He acted against the protesters, who were primarily socialists, with all the means he had and did not hesitate to have them deported. It did not come to an uprising in Lodz as in the Warsaw ghetto, where there was armed resistance; he receives the dubious credit for this. "Quiet in the ghetto": the King enforced this dictum with any means at his disposal.

What did we know about all that when we moved to the ghetto? We followed an order, we sought protection. What could we do but follow Rumkowski's appeal and trust in his administration? Everyone dragged along what he had. Bitter cold and great chaos prevailed. Children screamed. Horse-drawn wagons and carts caused a major traffic-jam; the richer Jews had much to take along. We did not have this problem. We pulled a sled with packages and bundles, all of our belongings, through snow that crunched under our feet.

The Germans led us to a large school, where a brutal reception awaited us. Hundreds of people sat crowded together on their suitcases, their bundles on their laps. With blows and threats, the soldiers demanded money and valuables from the Jews. Some hesitated. Shots were fired. Anyone found to be withholding a piece of jewelry was shot. We trembled. Intimidated, the Jews produced hidden valuables and money. Amid constant blows and abuse the Germans took them, demanded more money, fired shots into the air. Mother had to give up her Sabbath candlesticks, her last and most valuable possession.

We spent the night, two to a narrow wooden plank bed; others slept on the bare floor, some on their suitcases. The unheated rooms were so full that the body heat kept us warm. Suddenly we were roused from our sleep by orders: "Outside! Outside!" We were forced to go out in the snow-covered courtyard. They ordered us to let down our pants and relieve ourselves. Men as well as women had to squat on a beam. They forced the unwilling ones with blows. "Shit! Shit" they commanded, and "Laugh! Be merry!" The ones who didn't obey were shot immediately. Laughing, we had to relieve ourselves in the cold. They photographed us while we were doing it from all possible angles.

How could we bear scenes like these? Because we didn't understand what it was all about. We had no idea that the Nazis would use these photographs for propaganda; they would use them to prove that Jews were only vermin, crude and uncultured: men, women, and children shitting together and laughing. Already now, at the beginning of our stay in the ghetto, our senses were deadened by the Nazi brutalities we had experienced. We were stiff with fear. And we were trembling, with cold, and for our lives.

The humiliations were the first part of the strategy that the Nazis used. Before they killed us they planned to dehumanize us. We were to be tortured and driven into hopeless situations by our own people.

Through fear that we might not survive, our lowest instincts were to be awakened; by denying us the necessary nourishment and exploiting us for labor, we were to be reduced to the level of beasts of burden, until we died wretchedly or killed each other for food. Jews are animals, vermin, who could be killed with impunity; that was the message. We were to be adapted to the picture that they had of us.

In the ghetto everything was allocated: work, living quarters, food. We were registered in the ghetto school and were assigned an apartment. Six to ten people were assigned to each apartment. There were about 160,000 Jews assigned to 30,000 apartments. Very few of these apartments had running water. In the Baluty there was no sewage system at all. The building to which we were assigned was not large; it had a shabby appearance and comprised only four apartments. We three were housed with our six relatives in a two-room apartment of two hundred square feet.

From April 30, 1940, the Lodz ghetto was surrounded by barbed wire; the gates were guarded closely. The guards had orders "to shoot without warning" any Jew attempting to crawl through the fence or get close to it with smuggled goods.

On May 1 the Nazis assigned the German part of the ghetto administration to Hans Biebow, a former coffee wholesaler from Bremen. He and his men put the ghetto's production to use for the German economy and the Wehrmacht. The Jews' work was the Germans' profit. Hundreds of enterprises began to work for the Wehrmacht, from the carpenter's workshop to the saddlery, from the metalworking factories to the thriving Lodz textile industry. Belts, shoes, and coats were manufactured, harnesses, map cases and the like; the carpenters produced battery boxes, the electricians spools. From papers to brassieres, the ghetto discharged a steady stream of goods in order to stay alive.

"Our only way is work." This work was paid for in ghetto money, which could be traded in for food cards. The ghetto delivered the finished products to the Germans, who then demanded additional mone-tary payments. The ghetto administration could get this money only by confiscating valuables. Despite the strict controls by the Germans, new arrivals succeeded time and again in smuggling valuables into the ghetto. Rumkowski supplied lists recording the confiscated goods. In August 1940 alone he handed over five million reichsmarks to the Germans.

Actually the Nazi leaders saw the ghetto only as an interim solution. They paid for the delivered goods and stolen treasures with food, raw materials, and clothes that had to be repaired, sorted and cleaned. And they supplied people. A constant influx of Jews from the so-called Old Reich, from Germany, Czechoslovakia, and Austria, kept the ghetto population at the same level for a time.

The food supplies were insufficient. People refused the ghetto money. They wanted food, not money. If terror and the horror of losing relatives hadn't defeated them, now hunger and cold took the will to live from many of the ghetto inhabitants. The Germans' strategy had succeeded. Finding something to eat became more important than any moral law. Above all one had to avoid one thing: swollen feet, which was a certain sign of starvation.

No one knew beforehand what the allocated rations would be. Once there were fruit candies with the loaf of bread, then canned kohlrabi again. It was at the discretion of the Germans. Over time the rations became smaller and smaller. Eventually they were so small that it led to general enfeeblement and even the ghetto director Biebow sent com-plaints back to the Reich that the work force of the ghetto was suffering from starvation.

Soup! It was thin, warm water, in which cabbage, carrots and red beets were floating, with perhaps a bit of barley at the most. Everyone held on tightly to his bowl in order to ladle up the ghetto soup given out by the ghetto administration. People ate greedily, because hunger was the overriding imperative of life. One loaf of bread per person was allotted for a week, with minimal amounts of flour, sugar, and a honey substitute.

The children didn't do so badly. My brother and I went to school while Mother worked. Yes, there were also schools in the ghetto, because the former orphanage director liked children. There was no lack of qualified teachers, and under the Nazis' eyes we sang Zionist songs and read Yiddish literature. Each day we made our way to Marysin, a district of the city that was almost half an hour away. In the evening we came back to our mother.

Mother was lucky. She had found work as a maid of the wife of a very influential man. In the hierarchy of the ghetto administration, there were a number of people who didn't lack for much while the masses starved. Presumably Mother's employer was one of those bigwigs. Possibly he had just succeeded in smuggling a lot of money into the ghetto.

Sometimes we were allowed to visit Mother at work and watch her while she washed and cleaned. These people were good to her. It seemed she wasn't lacking anything, yet still she grew weaker, hollow-cheeked and pale. But she held out. Her goal was to come home each day with an extra piece of bread for us. Despite her obvious weakness, she scrubbed the floors for all she was worth. Having this work was a privilege which meant she had something to offer us. Her modest gold reserves had long since been used up. Had there been anything left over, the Nazis would have taken it away from her when we entered the ghetto.

Perhaps she traded some of the things that she received from her employer on the black market. Later I was told by a woman who had been in the ghetto that Mother ate almost nothing herself. She hid every edible piece of food in her blouse and brought it home for us. A piece of bread was always hidden under her pillow. My brother was always crying because of hunger, and when it grew too bad, she wanted to have something in reserve for him.

She urged him to do without the bread. "We need it for tomorrow," she said. But a child's hunger was stronger. We did not understand the adult strategy of dividing things up. They divided a loaf of bread into seven parts, as a small ration eaten every day was better than having to stand one or two days with no nourishment at all. How did we know what tomorrow would bring? And how often did we eat up our mother's rations for the day without even noticing?

Once—a scene indelibly engraved in my memory—she had a piece of chocolate for us. She measured it carefully with her index finger, as it was not very big. My brother and I each got half; she didn't keep anything for herself. Of course it didn't occur to us to share it with her. Probably she preferred it that way, because, without our noticing, she had long since been living just for us. She became increasingly worried. She had reason enough.

Rumkowski's ghetto announcements, which were posted each day, demanded that people give up the children. The elderly, too, were encouraged to come forward. The Germans demanded their toll of people, for resettlement, as they called it. At the beginning people signed up voluntarily. But soon rumors were heard that something terrible was behind it.

The Jewish ghetto police were responsible for fulfilling the quotas. Curfews were imposed; the police searched apartments, removing the sick and the weak, loading them onto wagons, and driving them away. Hospitals and prisons were periodically emptied by the Germans. According to Rumkowski's principle, the children and elderly had to be sacrificed. Young people and those capable of work remained. The Nazis wouldn't, he hoped, deprive themselves of the cheapest slave labor that they would ever be able to get. Where would this path lead?

What must Mother have thought when Aunt Mejci's three sons were victims of such resettlement? One day they simply disappeared. Had a commando snatched them off the street? Nothing more could be found out. Possibly they had voluntarily reported in to escape the madness of the ghetto.

At times there were rising hopes that the front would shift to the east. Perhaps the Nazis would draw back? One had to hope. In the meantime, having no consideration for others became a habit. Everyone took what he could get for himself. People collapsed on the street without anyone taking notice or turning around. The sight of someone dying on the street was nothing unusual. If one looked, it was only to see if he had something that could be put to use. A piece of bread, perhaps, or wearable shoes? We children didn't notice that they were trying to systematically condition us to not be human beings anymore. If we did notice, we didn't care. We were becoming hardened.

The latrines were always stopped up. Wagons with human waste were pulled through the streets by people and passed corpse-laden carts to which not horses, but half-starved Jews were also hitched. Pulling the excrement wagons served the ghetto administration as a punitive measure. It was the same as being sentenced to death, because the weakened human beasts of burden inevitably became infected by breathing in the fumes of the excrement. There was no sewage system, only cesspools. But even these did not suffice. People simply dumped excrement into the street. Swarms of flies descended on the ghetto in summer and epidemics spread.

The Germans demanded from Rumkowski the resettlement of all the ill, whether they were children or adults. The hospitals were emptied constantly. Those who had just undergone surgery, those with fever or deathly ill were torn from their beds and taken away. Rumkowski called on mothers to hand over their children and the older people, supposedly for resettlement. Nothing would happen to them, he told them. In order to survive one had to accept separations. If orders were not followed, the ghetto would be dissolved and everyone would have to go to the camps.

Raids increased on the streets. No one who left his house in the morning knew if he would return alive that evening. There was a blond

German soldier near the barbed-wire fence who arbitrarily shot into the ghetto and killed many people from a distance. To get home everyone knew that they would have to run for their lives if *Gingi* was there. "*Gingi*" was Yiddish for "the yellow one," as they called him. People informed one another at which part of the fence he was right then. Woe be to the ones who lived there and weren't fast enough. Many did not succeed in escaping his bullets. It was so bad that people who lived directly on the border of the ghetto dug ditches so that they could reach their apartments unscathed.

Desperation grew all around. Some people purposely ran to the barbed wire to get shot. Food rations became increasingly meager. Our little household was in bad shape. In winter 1941 there was no wood to burn. People burned furniture, but it wasn't warm for very long. Aunt Mejci was wilting beside us like a plant that did not get enough water. We hadn't heard her laugh for a long time. At the beginning we sometimes still fantasized about Aunt Ruchele's baked dumplings. Or about fish, chicken, real soup, a piece of white bread. Soon there wasn't even enough energy for that. There was no talk of celebrating the Sabbath; for us every day was a work day.

What could Mother have done? If she gave to everyone, then she would give nothing to everyone. So she gave her rations to us and took nothing for herself. One day her sister was so weak she couldn't go on. No vitamins, no carbohydrates, no fat, no protein. Only thin soup and bread. She couldn't conquer her weakness. She couldn't manage to get to her seamstress job any more.

One day she simply lay down in bed and died. The same was true for many others. I don't know if it was due to starvation or an infection. Typhus raged; boils and edemas developed on the emaciated bodies. Stomachs and feet swelled. Although there were enough doctors, they didn't have any medicine. One didn't enter the hospital voluntarily. The sick disappeared from the hospitals without anyone knowing where they had gone. Aunt Mejci's death was also the death warrant for her three daughters. Soon these cheerful little girls were gone. The last one was Idka, the seamstress, who struggled the longest against weakening. But one day she, too, disappeared.

"Our only way is work." This way was not open to small children and old people. Only those who were able to work were allocated food. Good workers were awarded extra rations by the *Jüdenälteste,* the ghetto eldest, at his own discretion. Still, Rumkowski called for the children and the elderly. "Before you stands a Jew destroyed. Don't envy me!" he cried in an address to the desperate crowd, from whom he demanded the delivery of 18,000 of the children and aged. "This is the most difficult order that I have ever had to carry out. I reach my battered, trembling hands out to you and beg: 'Place your sacrifices in my hands so that I can prevent further sacrifices, so that I can save a group of 100,000 Jews.'"

What a time to be a mother! The children were threatened by deportation, epidemics all around, nothing to eat, no heat. People let themselves go and didn't take care of their apartments, which became filthy; they simply couldn't carry on. The last piece of jewelry that they had smuggled past the Nazis and ghetto police was now traded for a piece of bread. Yet despite her hunger and weakness, my mother kept our apartment clean. There was almost no furniture anymore. It was always cold. I can only imagine how strenuous it must have been for her, weak and worn out as she was. She covered us with all the pieces of cloth she could find. She warmed us with her body, as she had done when we fled to Lodz. She struggled against desperation, exhaustion, and weakness, but she didn't give up. In the spring we planted a vegetable garden in front of our house. We even had a little tree there. With the vegetables we hoped to be able to improve our meager diet.

Despite the desperation, despite hunger, exhaustion, and illness in the ghetto there was an unbelievable will to live. Girls put on make-up and tried to dress according to fashion. Even though hunger gnawed, they tried to exchange food cards for a pair of new boots. Although they had long since lost their radiant looks, and their hair and eyes had lost their shine, they still did their best to have a pleasant appearance. There was love, even weddings took place in the ghetto, children were born. There were still many who did not give up.

We could see normal life in Lodz from the temporary bridges connecting one part of the ghetto with the other—constructed because we were not allowed to walk on a main street that lay below. Laughing children, well-fed and well-dressed, went shopping with their mothers. Streetcars went by under the bridge. On the other side of the barbed wire, enclosing Marysin, another part of the Lodz ghetto, you could hear the merry noise of children playing soccer. I was overcome with astonishment when I watched them. Why could they run around so freely? Weren't there any policemen out there? Hadn't I been a soccer player, too? I didn't have a chance to think much about it.

The raids became daily events. At work and on the streets people collapsed more and more frequently. Others lost their minds and ran around crazily. They were picked up by the ghetto police and taken away, we didn't know where. The newly arrived Jews were not used to the unsanitary conditions of the ghetto and grew ill even faster than those who were "old establishment." Hunger grew worse. Vermin multiplied, infectious diseases spread. Especially the lungs of undernourished people were weakened due to the cold and the lack of heating material. Tuberculosis became the folk disease of the ghetto. Every other person coughed up blood. Vehicles transporting corpses and the infirm rumbled unceasingly through the streets. Rumkowski demanded more and more human sacrifices on behalf of the Nazis.

For a long time rumors circulated that those who had been resettled had not been sent to work duty but had been killed. At the clothes collection centers articles of clothing were found that one recognized as having belonged to the "emigrants." At the beginning of 1942 rumors went around that deported persons were locked into the back of a truck and gassed with exhaust fumes. Mothers began to hide their children, families their old and sick.

Horrifying scenes took place. The ghetto police and the Germans forced innocent ghetto inmates to help them with deportations. People tried to hide. Parents were forced to smother their newborn baby, so that it wouldn't cry during a raid. The other people who were hiding with them in the cellar demanded it. But they would be found anyway, sooner or later. I myself watched a father smother his child in an attempt to save the lives of the whole group. And even then I didn't feel much. I had already seen too much. Up above on the street the Germans forced the Jews they had found to go along. "Keep moving. Move!" Only members of the ghetto administration were spared in the raids.

How must Mother have felt throughout all this? Quietly she took us by the hand when everything was all over and led us back to our empty apartment. Her master and mistress had disappeared a few weeks ago. As a non-working member of the ghetto the old lady must have been a victim of a raid. Now Mother was cut off from getting us extra rations. My brother cried and I begged for more food. She had to save from her ghetto rations which were already far below the existence minimum. She did so without uttering a word.

Mother grew increasingly thin, her skin transparent. Her cheeks became hollow and her feet swelled up. Still she fought for us. She didn't leave us alone. She walked through the apartment unsteadily. Every errand outside was a risk for her, yet she had to go out, for bread and soup. During the day we had to leave her alone, evenings we moaned about how hungry we were—although at school we got better soup than most of the population—and told her about school. She had less and less strength to talk to us, to ask us about what we had learned. She still sang her melancholy songs; crying and praying, she asked what would become of us. She still always had an extra piece of bread under her pillow. But she fell asleep earlier and earlier. Her eyes closed at nine o'clock, hours before the official blackout. She only spoke quietly now, saving her strength to hide from us the fact that she was slowly fading away. But she still gave us security, confidence, a home. She was still there for us.

In the summer of 1942 the number of deportations increased even further. For work duty, it was said. In truth it was to the newly established extermination camp Chelmno, where from the summer of 1942 on, 150,000 Jews were sent to the gas chamber; at least one-tenth of them were from the Lodz ghetto. Finally, in September, the ghetto administration refused to carry out an appointed large-scale resettlement. Now the nature of these "resettlements" was clear to everyone. Despite Rumkowski's pleading he could not deliver his quota to the Nazis. For the first time, the Gestapo and SS intervened with a degree of brutality thus far unknown to us. Sixty people died during the evacuation alone. Children were torn from their mothers' arms and thrown onto trucks. Many died immediately; those who lay underneath were smothered; others had broken necks. In the evening when my brother and I returned home from school, we found the streets deserted, the apartment empty. The little garden that we had planted that first spring had been uprooted. The radishes that we had planted with seeds distributed by Rumkowski had disappeared; the only tree, our pride and joy, had been pulled out.

The Germans had dug up our garden looking for people who might have dug themselves in, to hide. Now all was silent. There was no one in sight. We flew up the stairs. The door was open. The apartment was empty. Empty.

Mother? Mother? After searching for a long time we found a neighbor. What had they done to Mother? He avoided answering directly. Was she in the hospital? Ill? Dead? Captured? No, he hadn't seen anything, hadn't heard anything. Did we have anything to eat? A piece of bread? We ran back. We didn't know and yet we did know what had happened.

Fourteen-year-olds don't cry, but I couldn't do anything about it. The tears burst out of me. We both began to sob. My brother threw himself on the ground and beat his fists in the mud. September 1, 1942 was a gray, damp autumn day. It drizzled. Leaves were decaying. I can still smell the mold.

We began to call loudly, "Mamusha, Mamusha, Mama, Mama!" Our cries echoed down the lane. No one turned around or paid any attention to us. No one asked why we were crying. No one spoke to us at all. People passed us as if we were shadows. One often saw crying children calling for someone. Missing or dead relatives were part of everyday life and no one could do anything about it.

Disappearance was the rule in the ghetto, seeing someone again was the exception. People greeted each other with the Yiddish expression "But we meet again!" meaning, the main thing is we see each other, we are still here. We might weigh twenty or thirty pounds less, we might be suffering from swollen feet, typhus, and TB, have nothing to eat, and be freezing—"but we meet again!"

We never saw our mother again. Before we could pull ourselves together, two ghetto police appeared and took my brother and me to Rumkowski at Marysin. There as well, no one wanted to hear our complaints. "Our mama is gone," we cried. "Our mama isn't here anymore!" No one even wasted a word about it. They had heard the same thing too often.

Marysin was an extremely strange institution in the Lodz ghetto. In what was formerly a villa district, Rumkowski had fenced off a kind of children's ghetto from the normal ghetto. He loved children above all. He, who appealed to mothers to give their children up for deportation, had created an institution for orphans, where he hoped to make their lives as pleasant as possible. Children held the highest importance for the old orphanage director. It was them he wanted to preserve, to save when everything else was lost.

Directly next door to the children's ghetto were the villas of the ghetto's upper class. Rumkowski lived there himself. This allowed him to make frequent trips to Marysin. He allowed me and my little brother to go there. From then on we led, compared to our former existence in the ghetto, a relatively privileged life.

Approximately five to six thousand young people lived at Marysin. The elevated site, which was in a green area somewhat above and outside the smog of the ghetto, made a healthier life possible. There were even special schools, as there was an abundance of highly qualified personnel. Down below in the ghetto, university professors had to sweep the streets; here, at least for a short time, young teachers could teach. There were also Zionists among the teachers and we sang Zionist songs with them. There were gardening schools and nurseries; we could even take showers, an unknown luxury in the ghetto.

Down in the ghetto, a distance of a few hundred yards, people died in the streets. They were shot, they froze to death or starved, and were collected and driven away in carts pulled by other starving people. Up here we had extra food rations, allocated by the King of the Jews in his concern for the young people. We were clean and protected and relatively well-nourished, while down below deportations took place, and the King demanded the unthinkable of the mothers.

Soon after the ghetto was established, Rumkowski had obtained permission from the Germans for ten-year-olds to work in factories. As part of the work force he could better protect them from deportations. All the children had jobs. There were various enterprises in Marysin. I worked in the production of excelsior, my brother in shoe manufacturing.

In the evening there was no dull brooding about the lack of food. After work there were discussions. There was singing and we took walks. It was almost as though none of this madness had happened, almost as though we weren't mostly orphans at Marysin. A third of the lucky children were girls. Love affairs developed. Occasionally packages arrived, sent by unsuspecting relatives in America, and at least some of the contents reached us. Although nearly everything was confiscated by the Germans, we sometimes got a can of food or a piece of chocolate. So we were doing all right. We didn't have enough, but more than the people down below.

One day a beautiful, fourteen-year-old girl came to Marysin. "Look how clean she is," I cried, "look how her hair shines!" She was an obvious contrast to our starved and—despite our privileges—shabby figures. Her name was Lusia. She had red-blond hair and wore a long green dress. We crowded around this vision of loveliness, to get a good look at her. I felt a kind of brotherly affection for Lusia and tried to protect her as well as I could in her initiation into ghetto life.

We had relatively decent clothes, we listened to lectures, put on plays, danced, and even published our own newspaper. We wrote it by hand and posted it on the bulletin board. I don't know how, but I got to be one of its editors. The contents were eclectic: love poems to Lusia were published as well as the weekly menu and sports scores. Rumkowski was proud of such achievements.

The German camp commander Biebow came frequently to Marysin. Once he was accompanied by Rumkowski. It was a holiday. Lusia and I had written poems to Rumkowski, which we stood on stools to recite— naive words of thanksgiving in Polish: "We thank you, our President / You are our father / You make the sun shine for us / You give us food and drink / You take care of us."

Biebow was delighted. He came over to us and patted me on the head. Jewish bigwigs, the top of the hierarchy of the ghetto administration, appeared in Marysin on such occasions and showed their Sunday smiles. They were well-nourished and lacked for nothing in the ghetto. Later they were to share the fate of everyone else. We knew that Biebow was in love—or so they said—with a lady from the hierarchy of the ghetto administration. She was Mrs. Bursztyn, a truly beautiful woman.

He brought her chocolates and cosmetics. We sang mocking songs about the Nazi bigwig who acted like a love-sick monkey in front of us.

But when we went down into the lower part of the ghetto we met death. Killing and dying continued there. The gaps left by those who had been deported to the death camps or died were constantly refilled with new arrivals. The horror increased. When the clothes of those who had been "resettled" came back from the death camps it was our job to clean and sort those rags. But now it also was clear to us that the situation in the ghetto was taking a dramatic turn for the worse. The human fuel in the ghetto was being used up faster, the number of deportations increased, the ghetto population was declining more rapidly despite the constant stream of arrivals.

The Germans came more frequently to Marysin as well, to hold court. Six young people who worked in shoe manufacturing had exchanged their old shoes for new ones. For that they were sentenced to death by hanging. We all had to gather to watch the executions. They were fourteen- and fifteen-year-old children. Plaques were hung around their necks on which it said that they were Jewish pigs that had been caught stealing.

One of the six cried and cried; the Gestapo people made fun of him, and finally signaled the Jewish police to pull them up. The sight of these boys, who kicked briefly and helplessly in the air, the laughing Germans, the seemingly indifferent Jewish police, has never left me. Just as unforgettable is the fact that we came home that evening and felt nothing, absolutely nothing, except for hunger.

After scenes like that, the commander of the murderers, Hans Biebow, came around and stroked an orphaned Jewish child's head. When we got back to our barracks we were given a thin soup, as always, and everyone ate the soup and went to sleep. Our jailers already had driven us so far that food was more important to us than anything else.

A piece of bread and a bowl of soup. The soup was turnip soup, and if possible we wanted a portion from the bottom part of the pot, because there were more pieces of turnip there and more green vege-tables. The trick of how to get the thicker part of the soup—to get into the right place in the line so that the serving would be ladled from the bottom—that's what it was all about. Everyone wanted to be last in line so that he would get that thick soup. There was even a song about it: "Dear waitress, come a little closer, ladle a little deeper, there the soup is thicker . . ."

It can't be said that we didn't try. Of course we talked together about what we saw, recited the names of the executed, but what good did it do? We read, we tried to escape into a fantasy world as all children do. But food came first. That was the first step in the process of dehu-manization which would lead me to complete indifference toward life—my own as well as others'.

Even Marysin was not spared from raids. During one of these purges, I was in the hospital with a childhood disease when the SS drove up with a truck and cars and began to remove the sick children from the hospital. Roughly they tore the little patients out of their beds and beat them. Some were thrown out of the second floor windows onto the truck. I lay in my bed trembling, when suddenly a ghetto policeman by the name of Rosen appeared before me. He directed the excelsior factory where I worked and was chief of the Jewish police at Marysin. He grabbed me by my shirt and threw me into a room where a huge pile of bandages, stinking of iodine, ether, and pus were waiting to be washed.

"Stay here, don't say a word," he whispered to me, and pressed me into the pile of unwashed bandages, covering me with them, and shut the door. I had fever and was sickened by the stench of the bandages. The boots of the SS made a din outside and their commands echoed through the hall. Soon I fell asleep. I slept until the next morning. Then Rosen came along, opened the door, gave me a new identity card, and took me on as an errand boy in his factory.

The fact that he had saved my life was not clear to me at the time. I had felt danger and instinctively did not move or make a sound. I couldn't imagine that the "resettled" children were sent to the gas chambers in Chelmno or Treblinka. My brother almost lost his life on this occasion. When he heard the hospital had been emptied, he ran over and saw the truck driving away with screaming children. "Leon! Leon!" he yelled desperately and ran after the departing vehicle. He could only guess that I had been loaded on with the others. Fortunately the SS paid no attention to him. They could just as easily have stopped and taken the wretched child along.

That was the end of school for me. I went from one workshop to another, delivered letters, carried messages and goods. My name was unimportant, as the SS only counted heads and was interested only in numbers. Rosen liked me. Sometimes he took me home with him. It was nice there; within the given limits one could say it almost felt normal. Yet all of my friends and acquaintances from the hospital had disappeared; I would never see them again. The hospital was completely empty. Did that bother me? How was I able to go on as usual, even though I suspected what had happened?

Rosen was someone who helped many people. Much later, after the war, I visited him in Israel. He had succeeded in hiding himself during the last days in the ghetto and thus survived. I asked him: "Abie, why me?"

"Because I liked your poems so much, those you wrote for Rumkowski and recited in front of Biebow. Do you still remember?" Rosen told me that he liked my big eyes that opened so widely when I recited. He had heard me speak each time, as he was chief of police of Marysin and thus always accompanied Rumkowski. He simply had to save me. He showed me a small book. He had written down everything, even the naive poem of thanks that I had recited on that occasion. His son lives in Los Angeles and still corresponds with me today.

The job of policeman was a much desired job in the ghetto. One got good food, decent portions, but more importantly people believed that as policemen they could save their relatives from being deported by sacrificing others for them or by warning their relatives so that they could hide. For this reason, they tried to keep their police posts by any means and carried out every order. Here, too, the Germans followed their principle of having the persecuted themselves do the dirty work.

In July 1944, a month after the Allied D-Day invasion, through the end of August, the ghetto was liquidated. Only a clean-up squad of six hundred people remained at the end; in addition, approximately two hundred Jews had succeeded in hiding themselves. All the others were deported. Among those remaining were the Eldest of the Jewish Council, Rumkowski, myself and my little brother Shayek. The official director, Biebow, made a speech. He said, he hoped the Jews would take his words to heart. "Every last person must leave and everyone will get away." Bombs had been dropped nearby, all this was being done for the protection of the Jews, he said. Workers were needed elsewhere. "You want to live and eat, and you will. I'm not standing here like a fool making speeches and then no one comes." Everyone had to leave.

We went to the train. Like everyone else, we had packed a few belongings. I remember arguing with Shayek at the train station of the Lodz ghetto because he had forgotten to pack my favorite pen—although he had remembered to pack his own favorite possession—a small, flat pocketknife with a scissors.

The station was called Radegast and was only a ten-minute walk from Marysin; for two years I had heard the whistle of the trains, the sound of buffers hitting each other and shunting trains. Now we had become freight ourselves. Frightened, we carried our bundles and packages onto the platform. We had to wait in the sun for hours. It did not seem to bode well. People screamed back and forth, children cried. The SS wasn't interested in bringing order into the chaos. Finally they forced us into cattle cars by the hundreds and bolted them on the outside. Our destination was uncertain. We traveled a whole night and a whole day. The train stopped somewhere; railway workers tapped the wheels to check them. The car was crammed full; it stank terribly. Everyone had to relieve themselves in a pail that could not be emptied. We were not given any water. People died next to us, parched and exhausted.

After a long ride the train came slowly to a standstill. The dawn began to light the sky; a bright day began. The door of the compartment was opened. I took my brother firmly by the hand.

The ghetto in Lodz was dissolved by August 1944. Since 1940 approximately 140,000 Jewish men, women, and children from Lodz and the surrounding districts had lost their lives there in various ways, through deportation to death camps, through starvation, illness, or shootings. With them, another 20,000 Jewish men, women, and children from the co-called Old Reich and the occupied areas had also died. Approximately 5,000 Roma and Sinti (gypsies), men, women, and children, probably from Burgenland in eastern Austria, had been taken to a special camp close to the Lodz ghetto and murdered at the beginning of 1942.

The Nazis had power over life and death. Their Elder, Rumkowski, hard-pressed himself, played an impossible, two-faced game. He handed over the elderly for selection, because he hoped to save the youth. Although I owe my life to the existence of Marysin, I can't pass a final judgment on Rumkowski. I am careful not to glorify him. Some believe he knew that all the inhabitants of the ghetto had been given a death sentence; others say he really believed that he could save one hundred thousand Jews.

Did Rumkowski consent to be a tool of the Gestapo so that he could indulge his own megalomania and delusions of power? Or was he a radical pragmatist who would stop at nothing to save as many lives as he could in those circumstances? There is no doubt that his was an autocratic regime. The registration system run by his bureaucracy supported the Nazis' annihilation machinery. There was no law in the ghetto other than his legal judgment; the population had no rights. On the other hand, he did what he could for public heath and social welfare, and ultimately for the children.

One thing is certain: No one has the right to decide who can live and who must die, not even with the intention of thereby saving others. Adam

Czerniaków, head of the Judenrat in the Warsaw ghetto, took his own life when the Nazis demanded that he sign the order to deport children. Rumkowski gave the order.

The same train brought both Rumkowski and me to Auschwitz. There are various stories about his arrival there, which all result in the same picture: Rumkowski traveled in a private car, not squeezed in with others as we were. The ghetto director Hans Biebow had equipped him with a foolproof letter, with which the so-called important Jews could leave the ghetto. Although he knew better, Rumkowski hoped it would also protect him in Auschwitz. With his white hair and silver cane he was a dignified figure on the ramp in Birkenau, a person used to demanding and receiving respect.

Rumkowski showed the SS officer his letter from Biebow. He took it, tore it up, threw away the pieces, and laughed arrogantly. At a sign from him two SS men grabbed Rumkowski and dragged him away. No one saw him again. He was taken immediately to the gas chambers. They had to kill him; he simply knew too much.

Lusia was also sent to Auschwitz. I lost sight of her, but she survived. Later on I would find her again in America.

Concerning my early attempts at poetry: The survivors of the Lodz ghetto, freed by the Red Army on January 19, 1945, got to work digging up the ground as soon as it was soft enough to look for documents, photographs, and mementos that had been buried in boxes by the ghetto inmates. Supposedly, poems in a child's handwriting were found at Marysin, which are now preserved at the Yad Vashem Museum. I was never interested in them.

Hans Biebow, the epitome of a pedantic German administrator, had played a key role in the "natural reduction [of the Jewish population] through work" and had always been completely aware of its genocidal intention. For his lying speech alone at the ghetto's dissolution, in which he coaxed the remaining Jews to Auschwitz under false pretenses, he would have deserved the death to which he was sentenced by a Polish court. He was hanged in 1947.

. . .

I had spent four and a half years in the Lodz ghetto. I had lost my mother and all my relatives. Only my brother was still alive. How could we bear all these losses? The dead had become our life companions. This procession of spirits, I now realize, accompanied us on all our paths. At the time, however, we looked neither to the right nor to the left so that we wouldn't go crazy. We did not look ahead, as we were powerless against what was waiting for us. And we didn't look into ourselves. Otherwise we would have noticed that our youth was being stolen, our feelings maimed, and that the process of annihilation had taken hold—not only around us—but within us.

It was only by deadening the senses that it was possible to survive—by deadening all moral impulses and simultaneously sharpening all instincts of survival. This deadening factor makes it difficult for me even today to remember concrete things. True, I did have feelings, but they were feelings of numbness, of powerlessness, of helpless astonishment. Was it possible to still have goals in this condition? I did not have a mother anymore. I didn't have a family. But I had a brother. I had to protect him.

CHAPTER THREE

Surviving Auschwitz

Our train stood there for a long time. It must have been hours. The sick moaned incessantly for water. The stench could hardly be endured. We heard strange noises in the car from outside. Finally the doors of the freight cars were flung open. Air! A harsh light fell on the semi-darkness. Blinded by the glare, we climbed stiffly out onto the platform. We were standing on a ramp. The place had a name. It was the ramp of Auschwitz-Birkenau.

I still know what I saw but in my deadened state I felt nothing, except for a big, lightheaded numbness. Not even fear for myself, only fear that I wouldn't be able to take care of my brother. I didn't let go of his hand. Thousands stumbled onto the platform with us.

Figures with shaven heads in striped prison clothing shouted at us in Polish Yiddish: "Everybody out, everybody out!" The kapos pushed and struck anyone who didn't move quickly enough, pulled the sick and dead out of the cars behind us. I saw SS throw little children through the air like packages, saw desperate mothers run after these children, heard the rough laughter of the kapos and the barking of the German shepherds.

Flames raged out of smoking chimneys. The stench was terrible. Never before had I smelled such an odor. Bodies of prisoners were stuck in the huge barbed wire fence; their fingers, now contracted, clawed the barbed wire. "Keep moving, keep moving," the kapos bellowed. Soldiers in SS uniforms were everywhere. They too shouted commands. We barely understood German. They lashed us with horsewhips. Their dogs barked at us. Shots were fired. Mutely we clung to our bundles. I held on tightly to Shayek's hand.

"Put everything aside, put everything aside!" ordered the kapos. Now it didn't matter if I had taken my pen and whatever else was in our bundle. They took away my brother's last treasure, his beloved knife. They left us nothing. The kapos pointed to the smoking chimneys: "That's where you're going," they hooted. We looked at each other and didn't know what they meant. "That's where you're going, you won't need your things anymore."

It was a beautiful day. Nevertheless, enormous searchlights glared onto the poles of the camp fence. The shouts of the kapos were shrill in our ears. More shots were fired. Had I gone mad? I heard music. Now I saw it. An orchestra was playing. The camp orchestra was playing Strauss melodies on the violin and flute to welcome us. What could these sounds have to do with this scene? They told us only one thing: Everything that you have experienced up until now was normal. However crazy and horrible it may have seemed to you, it was normal, it belonged to a world in which you were human beings. This place is different. This is a different world. This place is a world of horror.

"Women and men form two separate lines!" Orders were shouted without pause. "Left, right. Left, right!" Smoke from enormous fires burned our eyes; we were sick from the stench. To the tune of waltzes, barking dogs and resounding commands, under whip lashes, shots and blows from gun butts, thousands of starving Jews took their places among the cattle cars as commanded.

They formed two long columns, five people in each row. On one side, the women with children, then the children and the elderly. On the other side, the able-bodied. We boys knew where to go. Weren't we able-bodied, hadn't we proved it in four long years in the ghetto? Less as a survival strategy than out of sheer habit we got in line with the men.

After the exhausting trip and the excruciatingly long wait at the train station, suddenly everything went very quickly. The rows moved forward. At first we couldn't see what was happening up front. By looking between the heads of those in front of us when we got closer, we saw an SS man standing several meters away from the first row.

Kapos and SS men crowded the columns closer together from the left and the right and forced them forward toward this man. He stood a few feet away, looked briefly at each individual, sometimes posed a short question, and then motioned with his thumb. To the right, to the left. We didn't know what this meant. Even by quickly observing that all children, women with children, and old people were sent to the left, and the able-bodied men and women were sent to the right, we couldn't draw any definite conclusions.

Weren't young women with children just as able-bodied as we were? We didn't know that the Nazis considered these children enough of a hindrance to doing work that they killed mothers together with their children. The mothers made too much commotion when their children were taken away from them. Mothers who were separated from their children survived. Some went voluntarily with their children, others saw them on the ramp for the last time.

What we didn't want to see was happening before our eyes. We knew it, we felt it, we understood it, but we didn't want to believe it: here was someone playing God with other people's lives. Whether or not it was Mengele himself, I cannot say. I only know that an elegant man stood there in an SS uniform, and that the rows of new inmates were steadily pushed toward him. His thumb motioned relentlessly. Without hesitating, he sent some people to the right and others to the left. A death sentence every second. A postponement every second. To the right meant life; to the left, death. This process was known as "selection." I knew the term from the ghetto. There, too, old people and children were selected for "resettlement." The results of that selection, however, were seldom noticed immediately. The selected were taken to the train station where they were loaded onto trains and disappeared. Here it was different. This was the final destination of all deportations. Here one couldn't have any illusions about a good ending.

As it happened, this judge considered us to be able-bodied; our lives were spared for the moment. With the instincts of a ghetto survivor, I had made us two years older. In the meantime, two cars from our train had been uncoupled, so there was a gap between them through which we were led. Approximately three-quarters of the people who had been transported with us went the other way.

The other way meant going straight to the gas chambers. At the time of our arrival, the train tracks in Birkenau stopped almost right before the gas chambers. The SS was proud that everything in Auschwitz-Birkenau ran as smoothly as an assembly line. The elderly, women, and children who had been selected for death were told by the SS and the kapos that they had to hand over their clothing and would be given new things after the shower. Showering should be quick and orderly so that they could have their meals as soon as possible. Some were even given a piece of soap and a towel. Most of them had no idea that they were going to their death.

"Keep moving! Keep moving! Run, Jews, run!" We others were hurried into a barracks under a continous stream of commands. "Take off everything, everything! Hand over everything!" We were forced over to the inspection grounds, in rows, accompanied by SS men and their barking dogs. "Run, run!" they shouted at us. We didn't have a chance to think. Not that it would have changed anything had we been able to think. In emerging into that other world there was no need for either reason or reflection.

In the reception barracks we had to undress completely and never saw our clothes or our bundles again, and went into the cold showers as naked as little children. We washed with cold water; all the hair on our heads was shaved off. We were deloused and were given striped prisoner's garments as new clothes: pants, jacket, cap, wooden shoes.

Then we opened our eyes to a different world, a world in which we were no longer human beings, not even human animals, as we were in the ghetto. We who were transported from the Lodz ghetto came to Birkenau when the extermination machine was running at full speed. It went so quickly that a number was not even tattooed on. Not even a number. And yet, we were still alive. We had been found worth sparing.

Worth sparing for the time being, at least. Before being put to death we had been put "on ice," as it was expressed in SS jargon. To be put "on ice" meant not to be sent immediately to the gas chambers, but to be given a waiting period before arriving at "death through work." The main reason for being put "on ice" had nothing to do with economic considerations or humanitarian concerns; it was merely because the extermination machine had reached the limits of its technical capacity.

One hundred sixty thousand inmates. Three hundred barracks. Four thousand five hundred guards. Six gas chambers. Four crematoria. That was Auschwitz II, the extermination camp called Auschwitz-Birkenau. This name didn't tell us much. Like most other inmates, we refused even to think about the existence of an extermination camp. Not because we believed Biebow's assurances or the lies of the guards and kapos. Even in the shadow of the crematoriums we refused to believe it, because it was unimaginable. It is well-known that in Auschwitz-Birkenau many Jews did not realize what was intended for them until after the doors of the gas chambers had closed behind them. Even then many still believed they were only going to take showers. Until gas streamed out of the nozzles.

The arrival and selection ritual fulfilled exactly this purpose: it didn't let us reflect on what was happening to us. The deadening of my conscience which resulted from that time still affects me today. It is not that I had to suppress the memory of the horror to be able to live. I purposely did not keep the memory alive. I deadened it further still, although it was clear to me—as it was to anyone else who went through this experience—that this memory would never go away. The fact is that even if I try to awaken this memory today to tell the story, only half of it comes to me. My feelings received such a shock at that time that I can't trace them anymore. Or is it that I can't awaken them, because I am afraid of what would happen to me, what would happen inside of me?

The Nazis had industrialized the process of murder and had reached the limits of this capacity. The greatest difficulty was no longer the killing aspect—an efficient method of mass murder had been introduced with Zyklon B gas—but rather the disposal of the corpses. In May and June 1944 approximately 10,000 people were gassed daily in Auschwitz-Birkenau. At the time of our deportation from the Lodz ghetto in August, it is possible that the number was even higher. The capacity of the crematoria did not suffice; no more than 4,000 bodies could be cremated at a time in the ovens of Birkenau. Seldom did everything work properly. Thus, the SS dug open ditches—115 feet long, 23 feet wide, and 7 feet deep—in which the corpses were burned. That was the stench that hit us at the ramp. Special Jewish work crews had to skim off the melting human fat and throw it back into the fire so that it would burn faster. Occasionally people were thrown alive into this hellish grave.

The disposing of corpses became a major concern for the Nazis as the pace of killing accelerated. Chelmno, Belzec, and Sobibor were constructed specifically as death camps and functioning as early as 1942. The labor-concentration camps at Treblinka and Majdanek were converted to death factories in the same year. Throughout 1943, the ghettos were emptied and their inhabitants deported to the death camps.

As the Red Army approached, the Nazis became concerned with covering the traces of their atrocities. Belzec was liquidated in late 1942. Treblinka and Sobibor, closed down after revolts in the fall of 1943, were plowed under and obliterated. The pace of killing increased radically at Auschwitz-Birkenau in 1944 as the Nazis rushed to complete their "Final Solution." By the end of June 1944, the Soviets had taken Lublin. Their discovery of the nearby extermination camp Majdanek brought the full horror of the death camps to the attention of the world.

We knew none of that, only heard about it in fragments, haltingly. When the kapos called to us at the entrance that soon we, too, would go through the smokestacks, we didn't understand what they meant. We still couldn't conceive of where we were, what Auschwitz-Birkenau was. For hours we stood in our new "uniforms" on the inspection grounds before we were directed to our places in the barracks late in the evening. There the kapos showed us why they were kapos. For no reason they mercilessly beat up one of the new arrivals on behalf of all the others until he bled, paradoxically demanding once again that he give up his valuables. They beat and kicked him until he lay on the floor whimpering.

Most of the kapos were criminals. Most were brutal henchmen who took orders from the Nazis, by whom they had been chosen with the eye of a connoisseur for their suitability as sadists. They kept order in the camps, for in keeping us under their heels they protected their own privileged place. The order of camp life was just as arbitrary as their cruelties. Anyone could be the victim of a violent act at any time. Thus, on the lowest level Birkenau was also a criminal regime. Sadism still reigned in the final days and hours before death. Leading members of the Lodz ghetto bureaucracy were now forced with blows to pull the excrement wagon.

Of the Nazis, it was the SS soldiers who used their whips the most; the officers limited themselves to the principle applied in the ghetto: for the dehumanized to dehumanize the dehumanized. Members of the master race of officer rank didn't even have to shout. A motion during selection, a quiet judgment decided irrevocably about life or death.

• • •

After more than thirty hours in a cattle car and a long day of hectic reception rituals and standing at attention for hours we were given a bowl and a piece of bread. After witnessing the first beating, a lesson meant to show us what we were worth in this place, we fell asleep. Our bunks were stacked over each other in three tiers. I lay down together with my brother on a wooden slab thirty inches wide within reach of the neighboring bunks to the right and the left. Lights out was at ten o'clock. I took Shayek in my arms, as Mother had once done in that dark room with the clock that struck so loudly.

We had hardly shut our eyes when we were awakened by shrill commands punctuated with rough fists. "Get up! Get up!" The bunk blanket wasn't allowed to go beyond the edge. In our hands we held our bowls, which, from ghetto days, we were used to never letting go of. Thus we were driven mornings into the latrines, similar to horse stalls, with no privacy. All had to relieve themselves together and to wash with cold water. One latrine barracks was available for six barracks. There was no soap, no towels.

I always stood next to my brother. I had to take care of him now because he had no one here besides me. An outside world had ceased to exist in our imagination. After washing there was roll-call. Everyone had to appear on the huge square at the center of the camp. Subsequently the prisoners working in the outer camps marched off in columns. For us there was no work.

The roll-call could always take on the character of a selection. No one could ever be certain at any time of when his life might come to an end, due to incorrect behavior or some sign of illness or weakness. The emaciated people whose bones could be seen shimmering through their skin were called "Mussulmen." Due to their weakness it was obvious that they would soon be unable to work; thus they were at the top of the list of the death candidates.

The food was so bad that we began to lose weight immediately. We still did not look like Mussulmen, but who knew when we would begin to disintegrate into that state? The water for washing was undrinkable. Those who drank it got diarrhea or even worse. Basically there was no other water. We were constantly thirsty. Feet swollen with starvation edemas were also a sign of impending death. The smallest wound could lead to infection. How could one treat it, if there wasn't even any soap, not to mention bandages? Where could one go, when hospital didn't mean treatment but only being killed more quickly? Every louse and bedbug bite was a death threat. There were more than enough vermin, despite constant delousing treatments. Each evening we checked each other over in the barracks. Each blister could be life threatening. The linen in the wooden shoes chafed feet swollen with edemas. What could one do about it?

We didn't understand the language of the commands, but quickly learned to read everything from our tormentors' eyes and to answer "*Jawohl!*" in any case. Even if we had understood the meaning of the commands, we still couldn't have grasped the overall meaning. There was no other meaning behind the laws and prohibitions than to reduce us to the lowest possible level of degradation. To steal and to be stolen from was the rule. Whoever lost sight of his piece of bread, his shoes, his bowl for a second had only himself to blame.

One had to line up for everything, to get one's share of bread, to get soup ladled out. The bread consisted of a ration of half a pound of old ryebread; the thin, whitish soup tasted like tin. In vain we waited for the thicker sediment from the bottom, turnips or greens, which we had sometimes managed to get in the ghetto.

Hunger was one of the most important means of our dehumanization. It had been with us since ghetto days. Some died quickly, some became ill via their weakened immune systems. Finally, as a Mussulman one could become victim of a "selection." Everyone knew: only with bread could one survive. Yet it was not just the will to survive which this hunger awakened. It was a furious, unquenchable greed that raged in the bowels. It was a feeling that smothered all other feelings. We felt nothing, only hunger. We would have done anything for a piece of bread. There were sons who stole bread from their fathers. The first thing to be taken from the body of the dying was bread. Those sentenced to death forgot their fate, if they were given a piece of bread beforehand. Better to die than starve.

Each day we saw people throw themselves into the electrically-charged barbed wire. In the ghetto "to go to the wire" had meant the same thing as "to take one's own life." Here, too, many saw no other hope for escape. Shots were heard continually. When someone ran towards the electric fence to commit suicide the guards fired from the towers and usually killed the person before he could touch the fence. One got used to the sight of people being beaten. It was so much a part of everyday life that one no longer wondered whether the beating was due to an infraction of the rules by the person being beaten or a whim of the person doing the beating.

During the day we had nothing to do, we just hung around. Now and then they let us drag a few rocks from here to there to see which of us weak ones would collapse under the weight. The idleness, interrupted by senseless lining up and counting off, by selections, in which anyone could get chosen at any time, this complete loss of the power over one's own existence led simultaneously to total apathy and suppression of what was being experienced.

I began to forget and suppress something at the same time as the crime was committed. Causing something to be forgotten was also part of the crime. The psychiatrist Viktor Frankl, founder of logotherapy, claims that it was possible to be a human being at Auschwitz. One only had to have the courage to do so. Frankl was interned in Auschwitz as a doctor, as an educated adult. There were those who were better off in the camp and those who were worse off. I, the sixteen-year-old Polish Jew, a worker in an excelsior factory in the Lodz ghetto for four years, orphan and protector of my fourteen-year-old brother, obviously belonged to those who were worse off. I admire anyone who succeeded in remaining a human being in Auschwitz and in preserving his dignity. Perhaps I might have been more courageous if I had had someone to tell me how to go about it. No one gave us courage. Courage was systematically taken from us. Why should courage interest us? We needed bread to get through the next selection.

One was never safe from selections. Who knew what the SS doctors were thinking? We had to run by them naked, walk past them, walk toward them. Time and again they looked at our bodies with their fleeting, haughty glances, as though something were visible, something that we hadn't noticed ourselves. Left, right, went the sentences. "Left" did not always mean death; sometimes it was the other way around. One never knew. People disappeared from the barracks. New ones came. We saw with unseeing eyes. We starved. In the night we held each other tightly.

Once in the distance I saw a group of naked women with shaven heads. Were they our women? Were these emaciated, bald ghosts our beautiful, beloved mothers and sisters? What had they done to them? One heard that in Birkenau many starved women didn't menstruate. What did I feel at the sight of these figures? What had happened to my feelings? I did not even ask myself this question. I had only one feeling: hunger. I had only one thought: bread.

At the end of September 1944 the unthinkable happened. A transport of a few thousand people left Auschwitz-Birkenau. Shayek and I were among them. Rysiek as well, a boy my age. We had become acquainted in Birkenau. He had come to Birkenau with his mother and father but left the camp with only one of his parents. His mother lost her life in the gas chamber. Rysiek's father was with us, a kind, old gentleman.

No longer "put on ice!" Against all expectations we had escaped with our lives from the extermination camp! Behind us the barbed wire, the chimneys of the crematoria, the black smoke, behind us the gas, the mountains of burning corpses. Yet it did not seem to us as though we were being saved. We were herded into cattle cars and transported to another camp.

The lords of life and death had their reasons for this as well. The Russians were coming closer. The Germans had to empty Birkenau, on the one hand, to erase the traces of their crimes. On the other hand, they had to cover the increased needs of their war economy, so they moved parts of the camp population to camps outside, to provide workers for the arms industry. Instead of being destined for death through gas it was now death through work again. In truth death was waiting in the form of infection, exposure, sickness, undernourishment, or shooting.

In Falkenberg there was no factory work waiting for us, as we had expected. Rather the SS forced us to to toil senselessly: building streets that were not needed, doing all kinds of work that obviously fulfilled no other purpose than harassing us. The camp routine remained largely as it had been at Auschwitz. Selections took place on a regular basis. We were given fresh clothes on our arrival at the camp, but it was the same thin, striped prisoner's uniform. There were no warmer clothes to protect us against the cold.

Wehrmacht barracks were situated in Falkenberg. A few of us were called up to work in the military kitchen to peel potatoes. For the first time I had the luck of being able to do kitchen work, an unheard of privilege! In addition it was a Wehrmacht kitchen, not a camp kitchen. There were girls in this kitchen, clean and healthy, well-nourished, with big breasts and behinds, shining hair and white aprons. They were ethnic Germans, and spoke Polish with me. When was the last time I had spoken with a woman? Our women and girls were emaciated like we were, scrawny ghosts with shaven heads and huge, dull eyes.

What could the ideal beauty be like for Mussulmen? I had never thought about it before. Our life was ruled by two things: get bread, avoid beatings. The ideal beauty for Mussulmen was fat women. Here in the warmth of the kitchen everything shone—eyes, hair, the fat in the pots, the fat on the bodies. I had never seen such breasts, such behinds before! There was the intoxicating smell of potatoes and bodies.

The cooks laughed, sang songs, and joked. How they moved! I couldn't take my eyes off them. In the steam of fat and potatoes something in me began to melt. A twenty-year-old friend who worked with me in the kitchen dared to smile at a girl. She smiled back. "Just imagine how it would be with her," he said to me. And I imagined it too. Suddenly, in the warmth, desire was also there.

"Don't look at me like that," said one of them to me in Polish. "The SS man is already starting to notice." I couldn't peel anymore, because I could not take my eyes off her. I did not desire only her but that other, clean, warm, oily world smelling of food to which I had once belonged, but had long since lost. In the warm, good-smelling kitchen, at the sight of the girls, I remembered it. I was not only a number, I was also a human being.

The thought made me feel as if I were drunk. Music began to play. It was around Christmastime. Outside the soldiers were playing and singing "Lili Marleen" again and again. All of a sudden I felt a longing, a pang, that I had never felt before. In Auschwitz I had had no feelings. In the kitchen in Falkenberg the numbness had begun to ease for one short moment.

A door opened, a man in uniform looked around the kitchen and saw me. "Come here, Jew!" he called. Now it's all over, I thought, still half dreaming, still unwillingly to take my eyes off the Polish cook. He took me along to his room next to the kitchen and shut the door. "Come here," he ordered. "Shine my shoes, Jew." What else could I do? I began to clean his shoes. Then he took me by the chin and pulled me up. He wasn't wearing his uniform jacket. I saw his suspenders close before my eyes. His shirt was green. Never will I forget those suspenders, his open collar. A Nazi soldier without his uniform jacket! Was he an SS officer, a commander or a Wehrmacht soldier? Without a badge of rank on the jacket I couldn't tell.

I had never been so close to an *Ashkenaz* before. I was used to scenes of horror. I panicked. He smelled of alcohol as he pulled his boots off. His green socks were also a shock to me. That must be an important SS man, I thought. I don't know exactly why. He had food brought for me. That frightened me even more. I didn't know how to behave. The unusual warmth made me so tired that I had difficulty keeping my eyes open. "You should eat, Jew!" he snapped. I couldn't.

Suddenly he bent down to me, very close. I saw the huge pores of his greasy nose. The smell of alcohol took my breath away. His commanding tone changed to complaining. "If you only knew, Jew! I have a son like you! Out in the Reich!" He started to get sentimental. In between he urged me to eat. Now I knew that I was finished. Soon he would come to his senses, realize that he had let himself go in front of a Jewish boy and shoot me. It couldn't be any other way.

The door opened, he was called outside. I sat alone before a plate that was almost full. Even now I couldn't eat. What should I do? To run away would be the end of me, to stay here probably the same. Then one of the cooks stuck her head inside the door and ordered me to go. Thus I survived this situation as well, which seemed to me more dangerous than a selection in Auschwitz.

I had not tasted his food; I was too agitated to eat anything. But I had a few raw potatoes that the ethnic German cooks had slipped to us: a feast! We didn't have any pockets to hold the potatoes, but we stuck them up our sleeves and in the turned-up legs of our pants.

After a few weeks we had to leave Falkenberg. Compared to Birkenau it had seemed like a sanatorium. Now the Germans drove us on with newly awakened fury. On foot. My brother and I found ourselves together with over 2,000 Jewish men, women, and children on one of those marches which was later to be called a "death march." An SS guard detail accompanied us. The camp system was replaced by the march system; one form of annihilation replaced another.

It was not the only death march in this period; everywhere the Nazis were emptying their camps, everywhere as they fled from the surrounding fronts they moved the prisoners, these living witnesses to their atrocities; everywhere they made these transfers part of their Final Solution. Now death was no longer concentrated in the camps; it was spread over the countryside.

Autumn nights can be cold in Poland. Forced to march in flimsy prisoner's clothing, with wooden shoes on their swollen feet, many people collapsed after only a few miles. As soon as one fell an SS man would appear with his dog and attack. Those who did not get up were shot then and there. We staggered on for a while, terrified of the dogs that growled, barked and snarled at us, but it didn't take long until the next prisoner gave in to his weakness. The shock we felt at his being shot compelled us to move forward again. It was a vicious cycle fueled by complete exhaustion. To give in, to remain lying there, to find salvation in a shot in the neck was a strong temptation. Dozens of people did not make it through the first day of this march.

For days the column of emaciated, weakened, demoralized figures moved on in this manner through southern Poland before it arrived at Wolfsberg, a camp outside the Gross-Rosen concentration camp. Of the 2,000 people, a third had died on the way.

Shayek had held out. We had shared a bunk as in Auschwitz, hugged each other to keep warm. On the march he was always at my side. When he couldn't go on, I supported him, put his arm around my shoulder for a while to drag him along. But one day Shayek became ill. It wasn't anything special, a cold, maybe the flu. He had a fever. He couldn't come along to work. I went alone with a heavy heart, but I went.

When I returned to the barracks that evening after work, Shayek was not there. Just his piece of bread—that half-pound square of dry gray bread lay on his bunk. Strange, I thought, that it's lying there. Why didn't he eat it? And if he hadn't eaten it, why was it lying there?

A piece of bread never lay anywhere even for a second. It was always stolen immediately. I saw that piece of bread yet nothing registered.

The other prisoners watched me, gave me sidelong glances. I didn't look back. I looked only at the bread. Why did he leave the bread lying there, I thought, we're always hungry. Why did he leave without breakfast? His bed is made—where is he? I ran out and called him. "Come on in," I cried, "Shayek, Shayek!" No one in the barracks said a word. They felt sorry for me.

Finally the oldest in the block came up to me, a friendly old Dutchman, and said: "You can eat it. Eat it!" Not until I noticed his commiserating look did I begin to understand. Shayek had been the victim of a selection. What had happened? Had he been sent back to Birkenau? To the hospital? They couldn't tell me. They didn't know themselves. It was pointless to ask the SS guards.

Shayek was not here anymore. That could only mean that Shayek was not here anymore. Nothing else. I refused to think that he was dead. I lay down on the bunk and resolved not to touch the bread. As matter-of-fact as this moral decision sounds, it wasn't. Why shouldn't I eat it? I was hungry! One ate the bread of every dead person! That was it. Shayek was not dead, so I had no right to his bread. By not eating his bread, although my stomach roared for it, I did not accept his death.

Exhausted, I fell asleep. In my sleep I kept reaching next to me. I reached out for my brother and felt only the empty wood of the bunk. Sometimes I touched the bread. I pushed it away. I kept falling asleep again, reaching for Shayek in my sleep, not finding him, waking up again. I sat up and looked around. Perhaps he was lying on another bunk? Perhaps he had come back secretly? I knew that he would never come back but I didn't want to believe it. I reached for him all night long. After that night, I had to believe it. He had disappeared.

"Get up, come outside, roll-call!" they yelled, bellowing like every morning. "Why didn't you eat the bread?" asked a kapo cynically and laughed. "Aren't you hungry?" It was a normal occurrence that people disappeared—the aged, the sick, the weak. No one ever believed that he himself would be affected. The older ones showed each other their bodies before roll-call, examined their flesh to see whether or not they would pass inspection. We were young and strong. Our feet were hardly swollen. We were very thin, but we were still not Mussulmen. I never believed that my brother or I would be affected. But now they had taken him.

Soon Wolfsberg was also evacuated. We marched on. Again dozens, even hundreds of corpses remained on the path. Again the SS and their dogs forced us through cold and snow, again shots resounded behind us. "Keep moving! Go on! Run, Jews! Get going!" Despite the icy cold they did not give us anything warm to put on. Obviously man is capable of adapting to outside temperatures to an astonishing degree. Nevertheless, many died of exposure, of hunger, of fever.

Instead of Shayek, Rysiek walked beside me. He was my age. It was good to have someone whom one could encourage and be helped by when one's feet couldn't go on anymore, someone to lie next to on the bunk. Someone whom one could rely on. I didn't have anyone to take care of anymore. Would I soon need someone to take care of me?

We marched to Schönberg. The SS herded us into a huge barn and bolted the doors behind us. In the distance one heard the cannons of the Red Army; the front came closer and closer. In the warmth we fell asleep. Suddenly shots resounded again, this time very close. We awoke.

Outside our guards raucously sang army songs. Through the cracks between the boards we could see their campfire. They were drunk and laughing and aimed their guns at our barn. We threw ourselves into the hay, burrowing in as deep as possible and didn't dare to move. Again and again bullets whizzed by us. The wounded cried out in the darkness. Their cries of pain excited the drunkards even more. There was no light. No one dared to move out of his cover to help someone else. Everyone was thinking the same thing: just one spark, and everyone who was still living would burn alive. The SS would never open the doors for us.

I only said to Rysiek: "It's good that Shayek isn't here so he doesn't have to go through this!" As though he might be better off in Auschwitz-Birkenau, or wherever he was right now. Nevertheless I was honestly relieved that Shayek didn't have to experience this. I was used to living only in the here and now. I had long since lost the ability to imagine the next worst thing or to remember something bad I had just gone through. We spent a day and a night in this barn. I survived it as well. Perhaps I survived because I couldn't imagine anything else. If I had known what I know today, that my brother had been gassed, I don't know whether I would have made it.

For the longest time I had been considered an adult, and had to work like an adult. There were perhaps thirty adolescents from thirteen to sixteen years old on the death march. Since they were not considered children they did not have any privileges. Sometimes a soldier broke down and slipped one of us a piece of bread. I had become strong and tough, without really noticing it myself. Solidarity had not developed among the young people, as the terror regime under which we lived only allowed individual relationships at the most. Many were dependent on another person—a friend, a relative. After my brother's disappearance, Rysiek and I clung closely together.

After the night in Schönberg, the remaining inmates of the Wolfs-berg camp—approximately 3,500 people—were loaded onto a train. Once again our train consisted of cattle cars, but they were open on top. The elderly as well as the young, sick or healthy, men and women, were all crammed in together. Some of the old people were in terrible condition, their beards were black with lice. Without food, without heat, without a door being opened, we spent several days and nights in a row in these cars. We had to relieve ourselves where we were; we did not get any water. Despite the cold, the thirst was terrible. When it snowed we could quench our thirst, but there was the greater danger of exposure to the freezing moisture. We pressed our bodies together to keep from freezing. Even today I consider it a miracle that we didn't all freeze. Dozens died all around us, and the dead were not removed from the cars.

Again and again our train would have to wait at a station. Trains of the Wehrmacht had priority. We never knew exactly where we were. Once we thought we heard Czech being spoken outside. Sometimes on such an occasion a train worker would throw a piece of bread or some potatoes into the car. We were almost too weak to fight for it, but did. Gifts such as these were rare because the SS and their dogs were constantly around the transports. Therefore, we seldom got a bite this way.

It was a sunny winter's day when we arrived in Mauthausen. The train stopped in front of the camp. We were not allowed to enter. The camp was overcrowded; here too the crematoria could not catch up with the number of corpses; here too the influx of prisoners exceeded the capacity of the extermination machine. It was very cold at the end of February 1945. Our train waited on the tracks for hours. Finally the commands came: "Get out! Everyone out!" They opened the doors. In each car there were ten to twelve dead people. We had to carry them out and stack them up on the ramp. Then we cleaned out the cars of dirt, vomit, and excrement.

After a roll-call on the platform, they herded us back into the train and transported us to our destination. After midnight on March 3, 1945, our transport arrived at the Ebensee station. The path from the station to the camp was long. It was the last and for many the most difficult part of the death march. Our trek took us through snow-covered woods uphill to our camp. Rysiek's father, who had survived all the strains of the march up until now through sheer force of will, was unable to continue. He died of exhaustion before his son's eyes. The weak and the dead, including those who had died in the open cattle cars, were transported into the camp on carts. They were simply emptied out on the ground in front of the infirmary, the living and the dead together.

Although it was long after midnight, we were lined up immediately for a lice check. Of course, we got nothing to eat. Since it had snowed off and on, our clothes were wet. Some of us had to wait in the snow for two days before getting into the delousing barracks. At night we crowded together to at least warm ourselves with our body heat. It didn't help much. People died in our arms. During the day, we piled up on top of each other on the inspection grounds so the warmth of our bodies wouldn't escape. When we rose up from the pile of bodies, the dead were right between us.

In all, the disinfection process lasted two days and two nights. Of 3,500 prisoners who had been loaded onto the train in Wolfsberg, fewer than 2,000 were still alive and 1,300 of them had been determined unfit for work. Many remained lying in the snow from exhaustion and never got up again. The weakest were put in a barracks without blankets or medical attention. The SS left their deaths up to the kapos. These kapos were often Jews who were rewarded for their disgraceful deeds with food.

The Ebensee camp could not hold more than 10,000 inmates. With our transport this limit had been far exceeded. Suddenly there was not enough food. The entire infrastructure of the camp had been thrown into confusion by our arrival.

I was among those who were fit to work and had to go to the former mining shaft daily. Originally the mining shaft had been conceived as a missile factory. Then the Wehrmacht changed its plans and decided to build an enormous fuel depot in the rock instead which would be safe from the Allied bombardments. One route to the shaft was almost two miles long and fenced in with barbed wire to the left and right. That saved posting guards. It was called the "Lion's Walk." Along the outside were narrow paths for the SS guards and their dogs. We took a different way, a bit shorter, but all the more torturous. It led down the middle of the village. No barbed wire protected us from men and dogs; we could always feel the breath of both down our necks.

Every day early in the morning we emaciated figures made our way between the houses down to our work in the shaft. The shaft was a huge construction site. While the digging went on deeper into the mountain, the inner walls were simultaneously being cemented. Several construction companies were at work in the shaft; their names can still be seen today on signs at large construction sites. We were at the deepest point where the shaft was being dug further into the mountain, and had to load the loose rocks onto the cart. We didn't know how to lift them, but we lifted them. Somehow we managed to push the cart. We didn't give in to the tiredness, the exhaustion. We simply kept going because it was all we could do.

Our guards in the shaft did not belong to the SS. They were part of the Todt Organization, Hitler's "chief representative for the construction industry." The Todt Organization was responsible for deploying labor, a cross between an official authority and an economic organization. In the Todt Organization in Ebensee there were older men who slipped us a piece of bread now and then, and gave us the paper from cement bags for us to stuff under our thin garments. That was forbidden, but it was excellent insulation and protected us from the cold. These men showed compassion, but only when no one from the SS was in sight. They were almost as afraid of the black uniforms as we were.

Evenings we went home from work, our limbs wrapped in the cement bag paper, surrounded by the SS and their German shepherds. The dogs were immediately on the spot with their sharp barking when someone collapsed. Anyone who couldn't get up was immediately shot in the neck by the SS men. They merely noted his number; no one was concerned about his name. We other prisoners had to bring the body back to the camp, where his name was taken down by the bookkeepers of death. Right up to the end, they placed great value on exactness.

Every day we had to carry one or more of those who had died back to the camp, although we could hardly move ourselves. Now I began deteriorating as well. Gradually my feet started to swell so that I could hardly take off my shoes. Exhaustion weighed as heavily on me during the nights as did the rocks during the day. But there were the dogs with their vicious barking. They sprang at anyone who stumbled. They kept us on our feet.

We staggered forward through the town. Left and right we saw picturesque houses with a yellow glow at the windows, where frost patterns blossomed. Smoke came out of the chimneys. Each of us thought the same thing: there are families in there, food and warmth. The houses in Ebensee were the first inhabited houses I had seen since Szczekociny that looked like real houses. What had been the houses of my last six years? Empty hovels in the ghetto with shattered window panes, dilapidated, cold, smelling of sickness, hunger and death. The barracks in the camps: stalls for cattle, not for people, an instrument of our dehumanization and brutalization.

That was the greatest torture of walking this path: after six years I saw a town again. These peaceful, warmly-lit houses bordered our path. It was dangerous to look too long at the windows. One could start to dream. If you dreamed, you shut your eyes. If your eyes were shut, you could trip. If you tripped, you could fall. If you fell, you wouldn't have the power to get up again. Then the dogs would come and attack you. A shot, and it would all be over. It was better to look at the ground and think about soup.

Sometimes we saw people. I mean people in normal clothes, not in striped prisoner's dress or in black uniforms. The residents of Ebensee. When mothers with children encountered us, they hurried on as quickly as they could. Once, it must have been during carnival time, we met a larger group of children. The little ones were obviously in a good mood, but when they saw us they became frightened. Mothers and children ran from the sight of us into their homes, as though we were dangerous criminals. God only knows what they had been told about us.

Once Rysiek and I came back from work, went into the barracks where the soup kettle was, got in line as usual, got our soup, and sat down on the bunk that we shared. A loaf of bread and a quart of soup, that was the allotment for one day and six men. Suddenly Rysiek had a crazy idea. He slid off the other side of our bunk and got in line for more soup. Another bowl of soup meant to live another day, to walk a bit straighter. Of course the kapo caught him.

They beat him until he was so bloody that he couldn't even lie on the bunk. I stroked his head, massaged his back gently to comfort him, smeared my saliva into the open wounds. I had a brother again, but I didn't know what to do for him. He clenched his teeth, writhed in pain, and cried out again and again: "I want to survive, I want to live, I don't want to die!" I only thought, why does he want to live? What does he mean, survive? I didn't understand what he meant.

No one would survive. We would continue to vegetate and then we would expire. I had not come to grips with death but I did not have any concept of life anymore. There was a Polish Jew in Ebensee by the name of Niedzwiecz. He was one of the cruelest kapos. He would beat someone up whenever he had the chance. While his bloody victim whimpered helplessly on the floor he would crown his sadistic excesses with the epigram: "People come, people go!" Niedzwiecz was so brutal that once in a while even the camp commander would call him to order.

"People come, people go." I looked at the two of us. Swollen legs that we could hardly walk on. I had a cough since Wolfsberg. Now and then I coughed blood. This weakness. Always hungry. Always thirsty. Always exhausted. At roll-call we could hardly remain standing. The walk to the shaft became increasingly difficult. It was only a question of time until one of us collapsed just like the others whom we dragged back to camp from work.

That was the end of April 1945. The worst month in the history of the Ebensee concentration camp. In April alone over three thousand prisoners died—more than fifteen percent of all those held in the camp.

On May 5 the SS called all the prisoners to assemble. Many of us had to support each other; some had to be pulled along because they could no longer walk. Ten thousand people stood there; more than 5,000 lay sick in the barracks. The SS men had come in trucks with their dogs. These dogs had been trained so that they always seemed to know when they should bark ferociously and when they should keep quiet. This time they kept quiet. Roll-call was dispensed with, something that had never happened before.

The camp commander, Ganz, began to speak and his tone seemed almost fatherly. He addressed us as "gentlemen." His words were full of concern. We were all going to be brought into a tunnel now, to protect us from the Allied air raids which were expected shortly, he told us.

He urged us to agree to this measure. We Jews, weakened through death marches and illness, would have gone along without resisting. Even in this situation we were still prepared to follow an SS man who assured us that he wanted to protect our lives. But since prisoners of different nationalities stood on the inspection grounds, Ganz's speech— he had spoken German—had to be translated into several languages. After each translation there was protest. Each time a few fellow prisoners—who differed from us in that they wore red and white armbands—sprang out of the rows and yelled: "Don't go, don't go! No! No! No!"

Ganz went slowly back to his SS people to consult with them. We lay down on the ground and thought, now the SS will start shooting at us with their machine guns. Nothing happened. After a while Ganz came back, and said it was our business if we wanted to die this way; they only wanted what was best for us. They would now leave the camp to go fight. The SS climbed up onto the trucks with their dogs and disappeared, never to be seen again.

So that was it, survival. That's how it looked. A truck, loaded with a few men in leather coats and with their German shepherds, driving off through the camp gates. On the inspection grounds the prisoners with the armbands hugged one another. The Jewish prisoners were too exhausted to share in the jubilation; we just lay down in front of our barracks and observed the scene. Whatever happened made no difference.

I had not understood what had happened. The people with the armbands were political prisoners. They were better informed than we were and knew what the SS had planned. We were to have been blown up, tunnel and all. To shoot all of us would have been too much work and would have left too many traces. Later the enormous load of dynamite that had been prepared for us was found in the shaft.

The "politicals," as we called them, were organized and informed. The communists knew which kapos had performed atrocities, who was guilty of which crime. They immediately took the law into their own hands and beat to death, stabbed, or drowned all the kapos they could catch. The guards who were old, some of whom had been recruited at the last minute from the surrounding area, stood around intimidated. They were happy that they had not been killed. We few Jews could no longer walk, could hardly crawl. We didn't want anything. We didn't even want to eat or drink. We only wanted to remain lying where we were. We hardly had the strength for revenge.

The "politicals" closed off our block. In the meantime, some prisoners had died of weakness. Rysiek and I couldn't take in any nourishment. I only knew that I lay half beside, half under a pile of the dying and dead. Nor did we really understand that we had survived, or that we could have organized our own nourishment. We didn't want to eat; we were too sick to think about food.

For one long day, nothing happened. There was not a Nazi in sight, the population was not to be seen and the "politicals" seemed to be in charge of everything. Then, on May 6, 1945, the U.S. troops arrived. So that's how freedom looked: two tanks turned into the camp filled with American servicemen. We still lay in front of our barracks, emaciated to the bones, incapable of moving or saying a single word. It wasn't necessary. The "politicals" took over talking to the Americans.

The soldiers jumped down from the tanks and brought us their jackets, their food, everything that they could give us. They hadn't reckoned with finding living skeletons. A GI stroked my hand, spoke to me, comforted me. He cried at the sight of me. He was the first dark-skinned person I had ever seen in my life. I didn't understand a word he said. Even today I am overcome with emotion when I see a black soldier.

The GI tried to get me to eat. I couldn't. Those who were strong enough to eat were unlucky. About a quarter of the camp inmates died in these first days of liberation from eating too much too quickly—the greasy canned meat, the chocolate, the cigarettes, beer, and Coca-Cola. The heavy food was like poison to their emaciated systems. We lay there, incapable of realizing what was happening. I couldn't move, I couldn't stand on my swollen feet. One could just as well have taken me for dead.

It took a day for the Red Cross to come and take us away. At this point I was seventeen years old, five feet ten inches tall, and weighed eighty-four pounds.

I can't remove the Holocaust from my life. But it is not my whole life. My mother, dead; my father, dead; my aunts, dead; my uncle, dead. My brother Shayek, dead, too.

The Holocaust is in me. It is that numbness on the ramp which I cannot overcome even today. How should I talk about Auschwitz? How can I tell the untellable? I must try, because that is where the unthinkable was done. I cannot fully describe it, only hint at it. I have a mental block.

Scenes of Auschwitz to which I have no connection go through my mind. The night when they locked us in the barracks, a long line of Roma and Sinti children was herded by. We heard them talking. We didn't understand a word, but we knew what was in store for them. The next day we saw thick black smoke coming out of the chimneys. How could one describe this blackness? And our empty reaction to this blackness?

How could I talk about feelings, when everything in me was in a state of shock? It hurts to have to admit that my feelings were more intense in the kitchen at Falkenberg than my desperation and my pain at the disappearance of my brother. At the time of his disappearance I was numb. Only later, much later, did these feelings reawaken.

Everything had to be pushed away, repressed, always. Repressing things became a way of life. At that time I couldn't and wouldn't accept that Shayek was dead. Perhaps, I told myself, things were better for him in the infirmary. Perhaps he had enough to eat. Certainly he wasn't freezing anymore. I tried to comfort myself. I pushed his death away from me.

Each of us who survived feels guilty that he survived and not the others. Rysiek was able to find out later from lists that Shayek had been taken back to Auschwitz with one of the last transports from Gross-Rosen and sent to the gas chamber. Soon after liberation I began to blame myself for my brother's death. Had I made a mistake? Would he still be alive if I had done something differently? I began to remember the little things, where I had not done enough for him. Did he die because I had not brought him enough potatoes, because I had stuffed my own belly in the kitchen? Night after night I talked about it with my friends. Could I have kept them from dragging him away if I had stayed there myself and not gone to work? Of course the SS would have taken me along if I had stayed, they all told me. I knew that they were right, but it didn't help. My mother sacrificed herself for her children's survival; why couldn't I protect Shayek as well as she had?

I wanted to avoid confrontation with myself, with this greedy animal that I had become. I did not want to remember. Every remembrance is pain. One can't tell oneself anything. One can only push these thoughts away.

On the other hand, the same questions come up again and again. Why were my father, my mother, my relatives killed and not I? Why was my brother sent back to Auschwitz and not I? Why did I survive and not my brother? Am I guilty because of that?

I don't know. I was a child until I ended up in Vienna. From that moment on, I had to be a man. A man without youth. Despite my lost youth, or perhaps because of it, there is one thing I never gave up: dreaming. They were dreams of a new world. Dreams full of "never again." Dreams full of "Tomorrow everything will be different." My life became a struggle with the past. I tried to push the past away.

CHAPTER FOUR

A Displaced Person

I close my eyes. I am lying in a white bed. It is a bed—a real, genuine, soft, white bed. I feel the sheets. They are real. After five years of wooden planks, freight cars, board and dirt floors, a bed as a sleeping place for the first time. I know it is a dream. I have never had such a beautiful dream. No fear, except the fear of opening my eyes and finding that it isn't true. Someone takes my hand. It is not the dark-skinned soldier. It is a soft hand, a woman's hand. For the first time since my mother's death I am holding a woman's hand. This dream should never stop. I can't destroy it by opening my eyes.

I open my eyes and see a nurse. I hold her hand and don't let go. She understands. She smiles, she leaves her hand in mine. Where am I? What has happened? Who am I? I am Leon Zelman, seventeen years old, from Szczekociny. I weigh eighty-four pounds. I am suffering from starvation edemas and weakness, and I'm coughing blood. I am lying in a bed in the Golden Cross Hotel in Bad Ischl that has been turned into a Red Cross hospital. In a real bed. It is warm and clean.

I dream on. I am wrapped up in warm blankets and brought into a neighboring building. It is a cinema. For the first time in my life I see a film in which people are speaking. Sonja Henie, the figure skater who emigrated because of the Nazis, has the leading role. *Sun Valley Sere-*

nade—that was the name of the film. I see that this beautiful blond girl gets what I have always dreamed of: she is adopted by an American family. Hadn't I always talked about going to America and being adopted? Wasn't that one of the hopes that I had clung to, as I was being transported in a cattle car toward Mauthausen when it was five degrees below zero? Or did that possibility only now come into my mind, as a rescue from this country of murderers, this continent of murderers?

Later I often talked about this film, and I have to admit that more than once I said aloud: "We arrive in New York. . ." That was Sonja Henie's line, as she waited for an answer to the question of who would now be her father and her mother. The girl lands at the airport; she is brought to the home of her new family where everyone keeps embracing one another. That scene touched the hearts of a cinema full of people who had just barely escaped death because we did not even know which members of our families were still alive. The open affection, the uncon-cealed demonstrativeness of these people moved us so deeply because for a long time no relative had openly and lovingly touched us, apart from fearful clinging in the night.

I was not the only one who began to cry during this film. Probably I suspected, as we all suspected, that we were completely alone in the world. The nurse said to me: "Leon, don't cry, little one, someday things will be much better for you." Still I could neither fall asleep nor stop crying. I wanted to go away, we all wanted to go away—far, far away. I dreamt the whole night with my eyes wide open—about America, about adoptive parents, about my sister Sonja Henie. But the next day it slowly dawned on me, that there was no one in America who would adopt me, an emaciated, tubercular boy, who had lost all his relatives, and whom they would not even let into America.

The nurse. So nice. So kind. I remained fearful of opening my eyes and finding that nothing was true. It was the first time in years that someone had caressed me and spoken encouragingly to me. When she gave me the thermometer I wouldn't let go of her hand. She understood.

The hospital gave us first-class medical care. They discovered that I was suffering from typhus and jaundice, which of course no one had diagnosed, much less treated. I had a broken nose from being hit. I had contagious tuberculosis. At least the edemas were gradually receding. I began to gain weight.

After three or four weeks, when we had been nursed back to health somewhat, I was moved with some friends to Bad Goisern. We were accommodated in two large schools, one for girls and one for boys, and still received constant medical attention. Now, for the first time, we could appreciate the surrounding landscape, which was breathtaking. Now we could listen to the daily ringing of the church bells, and feel sunshine and the fresh alpine air on our skin.

At this point the Austrians around us seemed friendly; there was even some contact with families. Whether or not they meant it, I don't know. I can only hope so. Political prisoners, who had been in better physical and mental condition in the camps than we were, believed that they had a right to material help and went to farmers to demand food. The Jews were much too intimidated for that. We didn't want eggs; we were satisfied with a little kindness and attention, a greeting, a kind word, a look in the eyes.

We had other problems. Slowly we became conscious of what was behind us. We had to cope with the realization that we were alone. As long as we were in the camps, we did not have to think of "afterward"; it seemed completely senseless. There was no afterward. What mattered was surviving the moment, not to become victim to a growling dog, not to provoke a second blow from a kapo after the first one, not to be caught swiping a potato.

On the other hand, what did survival mean? What was to come after it? There was no future. There was no hope. I could not even ask the terrible questions about the survival of my relatives, of my mother, of Shayek.

In Bad Ischl, as soon as we had revived somewhat, we crowded around a large bulletin board, in the hope of finding some news. We had all written to the Red Cross, which served as a central headquarters and search agency for so-called displaced persons and organized the exchange of information among all the Jews scattered around Europe. We were indeed displaced, misplaced, torn from our places and put into another. "Displaced persons" was a description of people who were far from their homes and were unable to take care of themselves. Almost 200,000 displaced persons—DP's for short—were in Austria after the war; more than one-tenth of them were Jews.

Meanwhile many of us had received replies; some found news of a cousin, a postcard from an uncle. Those who were healthy enough went on their own to seek information in Linz, in the suburb of Ebelsberg, where, in a large reception camp, a real information exchange took place. The jubilation was great when someone found a message from a relative. Yet many found nothing. Still, those of us who found nothing continued to check the board daily. And gradually, for many of us, the fear became a certainty: we were indeed alone.

During this process, a community slowly began to take shape among the survivors. Only now did we really begin to get to know each other. That, too, had hardly been possible in the camps—we generally didn't know the names of the others. But with care and nourishment, four hundred men and boys slowly began to become more human, to call each other by first names, and to see themselves and the world with new eyes. There were still occasional deaths from the effects of the concentration camps, but those were now the exceptions and not any longer the rule.

Our existence was based on the fact that the Americans were responsible for us. We created the basis for that ourselves by registering with American organizations and the Red Cross. I called myself Leon Zelman from Szczekociny, which corresponded to the facts. Had I said something else, it would have made no difference. In issuing our documents the American authorities had to rely on good faith in accepting the data given to them. This was how I came to have a false birth date, for as a matter of habit I was interested in making myself older than I was. This was a reflex from my experience in the camp, where children did well to make themselves older than they were, in order to appear more capable of doing work. So I gave 1926 instead of 1928 as my birth date. A nineteen-year-old has a completely different place in the world than a seventeen-year-old, I thought to myself.

The important thing was that now we had names, papers, and recognized identities. Anti-Semitic remarks were already being heard; Austrians, who felt that they were at a disadvantage because we were given more food than they, started campaigning against us. *The Salzburger Daily* accused the Jews of "getting fat and lazy, lying around, while the Austrian population starved." In Braunau, Ischl, and Ranshofen, mothers demonstrated against Jewish DP's who "drank up their children's milk." That didn't bother us particularly. We were too busy sorting out our own tragedy. We had to reckon with the fact that we were still surrounded by Nazis.

Next to our camp was a prisoner of war camp. People belonging to the Wehrmacht and the SS were interned there. They no longer wore their swastikas, but they still wore their uniforms. The close proximity of these uniforms, of those who were wearing these uniforms, was unbearable to us. As our strength came back, we remembered how the political prisoners at Ebensee resisted when the SS wanted to blow us up. Now it was our turn to say no.

We resolved not to stand for it. I was already acquainted with many fellow former prisoners in Bad Goisern and they elected me to be their spokesman. We organized a hunger strike. If we tubercular, weakened Jews would die from this hunger strike there would be an international scandal. We knew the Americans would be interested in avoiding that.

A jeep actually appeared from Linz one day, to pick up the spokes-man for these protesting Jew—in other words, me. They took me to the center of the American headquarters in Linz. I stated our viewpoint clearly—that we were still suffering from our recent experiences with the Nazis in the concentration camps and that we couldn't bear their close proximity to us. During my explanation, a young man in civilian clothing walked in from another room, listened briefly, and interrupted me in a brusque tone.

"You have to eat!" he cried.

"Who are you to order us to do that?" I asked him, indignant at his presumptuousness.

"I was in a concentration camp myself," he said.

"Then you should be on our side," I answered.

The young man's name was Simon Wiesenthal. We spoke Yiddish with each other as though it was the most natural thing in the world. Following his liberation from Mauthausen, he immediately began work-ing for the United States War Crimes Office and the Office of Strategic Services (the O.S.S.) A man named Einzinger, who was later to become president of the Salzburg Jewish community, stood beside him, a digni-fied older gentleman. He defused the situation by pointing to me and saying to Wiesenthal, "This young man must be helped!" Since he spoke English, he went with me to the officer on duty and lent support to my cause.

The Americans brought me back to Bad Goisern with an entire car full of food and promised that they would move the interned Germans and Austrians. And that's what happened.

These four hundred men, most of them young, recently liberated from concentration camps and discharged from the infirmary, had suc-ceeded in defending their interests for the first time in a long, long time. Now we slowly found the courage to face the future. Friendships grew out of acquaintances; we dared to develop affection for one another. It seemed possible to escape loneliness. Paradoxically, the feeling of loneliness had predominated in the camps, because we had been part of a dehumanized mass: In the face of death, which was ever-present and possible for anyone at any time, each person was alone with himself.

Now being alone meant something different. Although we knew it was very likely that we didn't have anyone anymore, we did have each other. Together we could discuss hopes of finding relatives again in Palestine or in America. Possibly this or that cousin or this or that aunt had somehow made it through. We had all lost sight of one another so quickly. By tomorrow the redeeming message could already be hanging on the bulletin board. Talking about these things was like therapy; in spelling out our hopes, we got closer to what we were really seeking— warmth and security.

We spoke freely, we freed ourselves through speaking. Now we could have conversations without being interrupted by the shouting of a command, without having to line up, without being beaten, kicked, or forced to work to exhaustion. Yet the more we spoke, the more we recognized that this continent could no longer be home to us. In Austria, in Germany, in all of Europe, crimes had been committed against the Jews. Here, in the shadows of the most beautiful mountain peaks in the world, murderers still lived. Here, there wouldn't be room for us anymore. "Far away," was our motto. And quickly.

Away from the memories. We were located—and that was clear as day to everyone—right near Ebensee and Mauthausen. We were living in the Nazi heartland. Hitler had come from Braunau. Many Nazis had fled to the *Salzkammergut,* the "alpine fortress," during the final days of the Third Reich. What were we doing here? The sight of a German soldier's uniform unnerved us even when his rank insignia was missing. We could not even cope with the sight of war invalids. We felt neither hate nor the desire for revenge. We simply felt alien. The manifestations of the civilian population irritated us far less than the sight of individual people in uniform. Under the Americans' protection, at least we felt safe from the anger of the populace.

So, far away. But where? To America! Yes, if that had been possible. I was suffering from tuberculosis and therefore could not get a visa. To Palestine? Perhaps, but that was more for adventurers than for TB cases, as emigration was illegal. The State of Israel did not yet exist, although there were underground organizations that were trying to build it up. Unlike the English who, even here, represented their interests as a colonial power in Palestine, the Americans in Austria tolerated this illegal emigration.

Envoys of the Zionist Federation came to Bad Goisern and offered a way to those willing to emigrate to Palestine: through Italy. Crossing the Alps on illegal routes, Jews waited for the transfer to Palestine in collection camps. Austrians also helped gladly, as each Jew who left the country meant moving the problem somewhere else. Some of our friends, having just escaped from the concentration camps, were recruited by the Zionist organization *Bricha* for guerrilla warfare against the English. One of them, Heniek Gonschor, lost a leg in a bomb attack in Bad Gastein.

Rysiek and I were always together. We hiked to Lauffen or, in the other direction, to Lake Hallstatt. Sometimes we took the train back to Ischl to visit our friends in the Golden Cross Hotel. On Saturdays, the Americans organized dances in Bad Ischl. Since we were the youngest, we peered over at the older ones, to see how they were doing it. Then we clumsily pushed the girls around the dance floor ourselves. An older couple, Victor and Regina Lazarkiewicz, took care of us there. It wasn't the dancing that drew us together; it was the touching, the closeness, the warmth. Many a marriage resulted from these socials.

The friendships made in Bad Goisern lasted a lifetime. Today I have friends from those days all over the world. One of them, Louie Linker, lives in Chicago. He has a family—a wife, children, grandchildren. We phone each other every year to talk about Bad Goisern. Recently he said to me: "Leon, you are closer to me than all my relatives. I feel like you're my brother." With whom among his relatives could he talk about those times, which so decisively marked our new life?

I had lost sight of another friend from Bad Goisern for many years. When I was in Washington, D.C., in the eighties and gave an interview for a Jewish radio station, the station received inquiries about whether this Leon Zelman was actually that Leon from Bad Goisern. Many of my companions there didn't know my family name. They called me Leon, or more often, affectionately: Lolek.

A short time ago, this same friend who found me in Washington sent me a large photograph. In it we can be seen standing at attention, like the graduates of a military academy or sports school, extremely proud of our new used suits and our absurdly colorful ties, both from American stock; washed, combed, and satisfied at being allowed to have a full head of hair and to stand straight and be able to make a good impression. We were happy about the growth of our hair and kept patting our woolly heads.

The photograph of my large family, taken on the field by the Pilica, is lost. It showed people from four generations and myself as a bare-footed, grinning boy. The photograph of my new large family would have to make do with one generation. Here I am a young man, smiling, and wearing a suit and tie.

These friends, who have made it to America or God knows where, connect their memories of Ebensee, Bad Ischl, Bad Goisern with me. We don't talk about the ghetto or the camps; we talk about the time afterward, when young people helped each other back to life, substituted for father and mother, brother and sister. There wasn't any psychological therapy. We had to help ourselves to grow up in just a few months. They called me "Chief" after they elected me to be their spokesman. I was younger than the others, but after I had gained eighteen pounds in the hospital I felt strong enough to speak for the group and to take over some of the things that needed doing as well.

There were many things that needed coordination: emigration, pro-curing food, contacts with the Americans and the population. I brought people together in our gathering place; I saw to it that communications functioned between the sick in the hospital in Bad Ischl and those in Bad Goisern and in the surrounding hospitals. In the hospital in Gmun-den, for instance, there was a girl with a bad case of tuberculosis. Her mother had been freed from a different camp and was searching for her daughter. I succeeded in getting the two of them together, and naturally I fell in love with that pale, delicate, beautiful girl.

Her name was Friedzia Friedberg, and I visited her with a few friends two or three times a week. Her slow death made a deep impression on us. One day her mother sat wordlessly by her bed and held her hand. The girl was dead. I brought the sad news back to Bad Goisern. As strange as it sounds, we experienced that sorrow like an awakening. After witnessing mass dying we found we could feel pain again at the death of one loved person. Grief was a sign of life.

It was getting close to Christmas in Bad Goisern. The group of four hundred slowly began to disperse. Of almost thirty thousand Jewish refugees in the area of Upper Austria, just a few dozen wanted to remain in Austria. Now I could notice the beauty of the snow-covered peaks. On long walks I had the opportunity to think about my future. My feet carried me as well as any other young man's. My shoes were up to each walk in the snow; if they had to be mended I took them to the shoe-maker. His name was Haider, I think. Only my lungs gave me problems. Once again it was clear to me: I was alone. But not entirely; Rysiek was here. I shared everything with him, even the fate of having tuberculosis.

Due to my activities as "Chief," some American officers already knew me. Some of them spoke Polish, which made communication easier, since I spoke little German and no English at all. The American military rabbi in Salzburg broke it to me gently that due to my illness I would not be able to get a visa to the United States. He advised me to go to Vienna. I was intelligent, I could speak. I should study. The

American Joint Distribution Committee,a Jewish aid organization, would take care of me.

What should I do? I didn't see any alternatives. To go back to Poland alone was unthinkable. I couldn't go to Palestine, I wasn't allowed to go to America. So in April 1946, almost a year after our liberation, I boarded a train with Rysiek for a city I knew nothing about except for its name, and the fact that wealthy Jews from the shtetl used to go to Vienna when they needed a good doctor.

Vienna, the West Train Station! There was no train station. There was no arrival hall. The bombs had left nothing standing. The first impression of this city, after all the fresh natural beauty of the Salzkammergut, was depressing and gray. But we were in Vienna.

The square in front of the station was also destroyed. Rysiek and I stood there and digested the scene. People, people, people. No street, only temporary footbridges, boards, which one had to use to cross over the street. Soldiers. Automobile traffic. Ringing streetcars, crowded with people. Shopkeepers. Enormous buildings and in between them gaping bomb craters.

Had I not stood like this once before and observed a city? This time the swastika flags were missing, marching Hitler Youth were nowhere to be seen; instead of the Nazis, Allied soldiers promenaded by with garishly painted girls on their arms. A sharp desire came over me to succeed, to make my way here in Vienna. Here on this square, a fierce urge took hold of me to get back what had been taken from me for six long years.

Vienna. I knew nothing of this city. Nothing about Hitler saying it was a pearl that he wanted to make a setting for. Nothing about the fact that before the rise of the Nazis, the Jewish community had numbered almost 180,000. Nothing about the over 65,000 Jews from Vienna who had died in the Nazis' camps. Only 4,000 people who were Jews according to the Nüremberg Laws still lived there in 1945; a third of them had been baptized. The rest of them left as soon as they could.

Although we knew nothing about Vienna, it constituted our third-best hope. Vienna was full of refugees, full of people who had escaped the camps, but also those fleeing from the new regimes in the East. Vienna, a transient city, Austria, a transient country. Between 1945 and 1948 a million people passed through this revolving door; one-tenth of them were Jews. The Jewish refugees considered Vienna the gateway to the West, to America, to Palestine.

On the other hand, the Western aid organizations had their Eastern-most bases in Vienna, because they considered Vienna to be their window to the East. The four occupying powers additionally gave Vienna the flair of an international city. They also guaranteed that a diplaced person such as myself felt safer in the city than in the country. Vienna, the open city.

Many Jews came to Vienna, because here large reception centers existed, such as the Rothschild Hospital. Others were just too tired to go any further. Still others, like us, could not go anywhere else but lived as DP's on American aid. The idea did not even occur to us that we might awaken the envy of the Austrian population, as we didn't make a single demand on the Austrian taxpayer. To most Austrians, however, this consideration mattered as little as did our past history. They envied us for the support we got, without wanting to know what we had gone through. They saw us primarily as a foreigner problem, and one that reminded them of the recent past which was beginning to be repressed all around.

The aid organization, the American Joint Distribution Committee, took care of our material needs. The Joint was the largest Jewish aid organization in America. They concerned themselves with the fate of all Jewish refugees and DP's and helped with the reconstruction of Jewish communities all over Europe. The Joint supplied us with food and clothing, gave us a little money, and provided an apartment for us. We called ourselves "Children of the Joint."

A care package came once a month. It measured approximately sixteen inches square and almost as high—an impressive box. We kept a bar of chocolate and a can of sweetened condensed milk for ourselves. At night when we couldn't sleep we licked the thick, sweet sauce out of the can. It calmed us like mother's milk. The cigarette packages we saved for special opportunities—a useful object for trading.

Once I traded pants sewn from a blanket for two packs of cigarettes. The clothing from the collection centers gave us the appearance of clowns; if possible, we wanted to dress ourselves better. The package of cheese from the care package had the brand name "Kraft." We gave it away as we did the salty crackers and the canned corned beef. One could provide happiness with such gifts. One could also buy affection. We were still as addicted to affection as on the first day of liberation. Perhaps even more addicted, because we had more strength to wish for it.

Still we suffered from hunger, as did most of the people around us. The care packages made our lives easier, but they did not make us full. The Joint supported us with a modest stipend. But with money one could not always get food; here one had to have food stamps. On the other hand, a cigarette could move a waiter to make an exception and, in the cheaper restaurants that we frequented, to exchange soup for money.

With my friend Rysiek I first shared a tiny apartment on Untere Augartenstrasse. I let him have the bed and I slept in the bathtub. A bit later we moved to Kaindlgasse in the seventh district, then into a furnished room at Liechtensteinstrasse 20. A lady lived there who called herself a countess. Her domain consisted of her large apartment, which she rented to black soldiers by the hour. We made friends with the girls; they were very nice to us, once one even embraced me. I couldn't enjoy it, however, as I was afraid that her boyfriend would catch me. He lay drunk in his room, thank God. Nevertheless, we kept a respectful distance from the heavily-built GI's.

Then we were lucky and an old lady made a relatively large apartment available to us at Rudolfsplatz. Each of us had his own room! The balcony with a view of the inner city seemed very impressive. Of course we used our residence to make an impression on girls. I already had a girlfriend named Erika. Her father was never at home but her mother sometimes cooked for us, so there was almost a touch of family life. They lived on Hörlgasse in the ninth district. At Christmas I brought them my whole care package, to contribute to a nice celebration. For me, Christmas was not a religious occasion, but it brought back the remembrance of family festivities in general.

So I went to the family on Christmas Eve. Many other guests were there. I noticed immediately that my friend's mother tried to keep me away from a certain man, a large brawny type. The evening took its course, there was drinking, some people had brought along wine. Suddenly the brawny one, Erika's uncle, spoke to me. I didn't speak much German yet. We conversed a bit, but Erika came over quickly and tried to pull him away. He would not let himself be dissuaded from talking with me. He was visibly tipsy.

"Where do you come from?" he asked me.

"From Poland."

"Where?"

"From Lodz."

"What do you mean Lodz? It's called Litzmannstadt!" He seemed to think that I was an ethnic German.

"We did good work there, kicked the Jews' asses, really warmed them up nicely, don't you think?"

The lady of the house turned red with embarrassment. Together with her daughter, she tried to silence the old uncle. I had just come out of captivity, she said, I needed to be treated gently, I didn't want to hear about those things. In vain.

"But I have to tell my young friend how we made things hot for the Jews!"

I fled. Ran out of the apartment, down the stairs. It was ice-cold outside. Erika and her mother followed me, tried to catch up, called after me. I heard them but I didn't stop. I ran straight to Rudolfsplatz, upstairs to my apartment, threw myself on the bed. I never saw the girl and her mother again. I was sorry, because I liked both of them, but I didn't want to have anything to do with those people.

We were busy preparing for the Matura, the Austrian graduation exams from secondary school. In the late afternoon, we went to school in the eighth district. During the day we took language courses offered by the Joint at its headquarters on Währingerstrasse. I told a schoolmate at the Matura preparation class about my Christmas experience. He didn't say anything at first, weighing his words for a long time. "What can I tell you? That's how we were, that's how they all are," he finally answered.

Fritz, my schoolmate, was not a Jew. He was a bit older than I. He had been with the Hitler Youth and had then lost an arm in the war. At school we had soldiers in our class who had been drafted into the Austrian army and also had not finished school. Fritz was one of those soldiers. Although we had put up a fight against having war criminals so close by in Bad Goisern, we couldn't do anything about it here. Finally, it became obvious that they were not all criminals. There it was: the first encounter with the other side, with the other world, here on a school bench in the Matura preparation class in the eighth district.

I didn't know anything about these ex-soldiers. I felt only an unconquerable revulsion for them. Fritz knew very little about the fate of the Jews. Or did he know too much? In any case, in a quiet way he made himself indispensable to me at school.

Anyone who had observed this pale, thin young man would have to have called him reserved. I didn't fail to notice his constant presence. Spellbound I stared at the empty arm of his jacket. "What does he want?" I thought to myself. "Serves him right with his hand, why did he have to go to war against other people." And even if he noticed my revulsion, he did not give up. When I looked for a book, Fritz had it right there. When I could not do some work, Fritz was there and found the answer. When I didn't know how to pronounce a word, Fritz told me how.

It was nice for me to have someone to help me study. As time went on my curiosity outweighed my revulsion, and in the evening I looked forward to seeing him the next afternoon. So we got to talking. He sought my eyes, talked falteringly about the Nazi regime. This report from the other side fascinated me; I had the impression that Fritz wanted to justify himself, as if he did not want my pity, but my understanding.

Mixed with my revulsion I felt a strange satisfaction that a Hitler Youth was speaking to me like this. Whenever I spoke with him, something inside me fought against it at the same time. It said to me: "If he is so good today, how could he have been a criminal yesterday?" At the time, I knew very little about the Wehrmacht and their role in Nazi atrocities.

We stayed in touch for years. Later he told me about his wedding, then about his divorce, and finally we lost track of one another. He never spoke about his father. I always suspected that he had been a high-ranking Nazi. Once when I was invited to his home, his father didn't appear and his mother did not speak of her husband. Once Fritz intimated that he had been so blinded by the Nazis that as an eighteen-year-old he had signed up for the most active front.

There was always a light veil of mistrust between us, especially after the Christmas Eve I celebrated at Erika's. I would have liked to give him chocolate or cigarettes, but I didn't want to offend him, show him that a Jewish youth possessed more than he did. On the other hand, I had the feeling that he wanted to do something for me, to make amends, to apologize. He gave me the book *Red-White-Red* with the words inscribed: "This is now our common homeland." He failed to notice that in this book, there is only talk of Austria's role as a victim of Hitlerism but nothing about the Jews. Our curiosity about the strangeness of the other attracted us; nevertheless, he lacked the courage for friendship and my prejudices were in the way.

My prejudices evolved from personal experiences. Massive anti-Semitism prevailed in Vienna. A poll showed that forty-six percent of the population had anti-Semitic feelings. Refugees and DP's were unwelcome guests. The *Arbeiter-Zeitung*, the labor newspaper, summarized the mood in a headline: "We want to be rid of them!" There was no way one could not be aware of all that. Yet, strange as it may sound, I didn't take it personally. I pushed it aside, so that I could build my own world. For me, what was in the newspaper didn't count. Only my personal encounters mattered.

We young Jews only really felt safe and free when we were among ourselves. We were three friends: Rysiek, who had a much worse case of tuberculosis than I, and spent weeks in a sanatorium in Davos. He had become bitter from what he had experienced. At least I had been spared seeing my relatives die. Rysiek and I needed each other like two brothers. Indeed, he replaced Shayek for me. We were everything to one another, shared everything with each other, knew everything about each other. Frante Spitzer was the third in our group. He was a young Slovak who had lost his mother in a camp in Minsk, his father in Flossenbürg. He returned to Brno in 1945, quickly finished his Matura, and had come to Vienna to become an interpreter.

Frante was sophisticated and skilled at languages; he was able to find his way anywhere. He gave German lessons to Russians as well as Americans. We became acquainted with him immediately after our arrival. He became our cicerone in postwar Vienna, opening many new worlds to us. He had already started studying and was one of the founders of the Association of Jewish University Students. We got into these circles through him, although we were still only studying for the Matura. The beautiful singer Erika Wien, later his wife, was always at his side, and Frante found a family again with her and her parents. In the world of art, Frante was also at home.

We had our own Viennese topography. Our neighborhood was the second district, the Leopoldstadt. This was the Russian Zone, where several Jewish institutions were situated, among them the most important one for us, the Joint's food kitchen on Kleine Pfarrgasse. The spacious, clean cafeteria served as a meeting place. We also liked to meet in a small tavern on Obere Augartenstrasse, where for just a little money we could sit and exchange news.

Daily we trudged over the Augarten Bridge into the first district, the International Zone. There, on Seitenstettengasse, was the clothing distribution center for the Jewish community of Vienna. Rysiek's and my first apartment had been at Rudolfsplatz. When we left the International Zone in the other direction we came to the American Zone. In the eighth district we went to school; in the ninth, at Währingerstrasse 4, was the central office of the Joint, where we had our language courses. Also in the ninth, on Pramergasse, was the place of our constant desire; the large food warehouse of the Joint which opened its doors to us. There we got matzoh, canned fruit, cookies, sugar, and other delicacies. On Passover the American military rabbi even organized seders for us, with matzoh and all the special dishes to remind us of the exodus from Egypt.

Hotel Regina was located near the university. In its cheap cafeteria, which was open to the public, the waiters already knew us and were prepared to do some trading—cigarettes for food. The athletes of the Jewish sports club, Hakoah, which was reestablished, met in the seventh district, at Café Blumenfeld on Urban-Loritz-Platz. Our interest in sports was not based so much on the desire for competition; it was rather an excuse for going out together after practice. Even though the athletes did their best to revive the legendary soccer team, the team did not succeed in the long run. Purim parties and gatherings of all sorts at Café Blumenfeld compensated enough.

These four or five districts represented a kind of home territory among the ruins. Nevertheless, Vienna was and remained only a substitute for me, a temporary solution. I was here only because they had not let me into America. But I was starved for people; I sought encounters, friends, lovers. At the same time Vienna was a place of despair. My thoughts kept returning to the question: What am I supposed to do here?

I still knew nothing about this city. I knew only one thing: here they spoke the language of our tormentors. This was the country where Hitler was born. This was a Hitler city. Nazis sat in every coffeehouse, in every tavern. One had to be aware that at anytime one could meet up with one's brother's murderer, and not even know it.

We were here, but whether we belonged here was something we were unsure of for a long time. At least we had each other. Together we were building the framework of a village in this large city; we tried not merely to exist but to shape a life. Each year on May 6, on the anniversary of our liberation, we sat down together, placed a loaf of bread on the table, and ate until we were full.

Despite the beginnings of a community, many young Jews still had their point of refuge outside this city. They looked toward Palestine. Building up the Jewish State, winning its independence, planning their emigration made their life bearable for them. Others hoped to be able to emigrate to America after finishing up their professional education. I didn't have this hope. I had to create another point of refuge for myself.

What would have seemed to be an absurd idea at my first sight of the city now began to take shape. I experienced the fever of reconstruction, saw the buildings growing out of gaps, bridges that began to stretch over the Danube Canal. Rubble was being cleared away, followed by rebuilding, everywhere. Everyone around us seemed to be looking ahead.

Tuberculosis and depression seemed to go hand in hand. Some of us couldn't bear being alone for one second. If they didn't have anyone to be with, they bought themselves girls to keep from being alone. Many got married for this reason. Alone they would have perished. I often had fits of crying during the night. I still blamed myself for my brother's death. Without thinking about it, I created a point of refuge in myself. I spoke with my mother. I shared each success with her. The main motivation for passing exams was so that I could tell her about it. She should be proud of her son; only when I felt she was proud of me, could I be proud of myself.

Today I recall that in all of the ghetto and camp years we were subject to strict organization, a totalitarian system where everything was organized and planned for us. In Bad Ischl and Bad Goisern as well life followed the pattern of a large crowd of people who all have to be nourished and accommodated. Now everything was different. Now we were alone. True, the Joint and the Red Cross looked after us, but no one determined the course of our lives. Freedom was too much for many of us, to have to exist alone in a city of millions. I stepped from an organized life into having to organize my own life.

I walked through the streets and observed people's faces. Which ones could be trusted, which not? Where could I make friends, where could I help, where could I get help, where could I find love and community? There were the Russians. They didn't scare me. It was obvious to me that without them there would not have been a victory over Hitler. Although I had picked up the word and the feeling surrounding the word in the shtetl, I had no idea what socialism was. But in Vienna I intuitively grasped that the Russians were not evil. They saw that we were Jews, patted us on the back when we walked down the Grosse Pfarrgasse, called to us encouragingly, "Evrej, Evrej!" and sought our company. They invited us to the officers' mess in the Hofburg, to their dances in the Volksgarten, and some spoke Yiddish with us.

They took us along to films in the Tabor Cinema. Together we sang songs about Stalin, the liberator. He *had* liberated us, hadn't he? The advance of the Red Army had saved the lives of thousands of concentration camp inmates at the last minute. The Russians had sacrificed their lives to liberate Vienna. To me they were no different from that black GI who had stroked my hand in Ebensee and cried over me. What did we know of Stalin's show trials, the executions, the Gulag? The Soviet Union was something we accepted. Politically I was completely naive. Many Jews, like me, developed sympathy for the Russians and for Communism simply out of gratitude.

The squabbles of the official Jewish Community were beyond our comprehension. We knew that the first president of the Community, David Brill—who was appointed in 1945 by the Austrian Minister of Education, Ernst Fischer—was a Communist, but that meant nothing to us. We also didn't notice that there were strong tendencies against the reconstruction of a Jewish community in Vienna. The World Jewish Congress was the strongest legitimate political organization of all Jews prior to Israel becoming a state, and its representatives were of the opinion after 1945 that Jews should never again settle in Germany and Austria. Naturally, lacking alternatives, my opinion was completely different. Later, however, I was to have it out with the religious community on this question. And much later, the World Jewish Congress was to play a very different role in my life.

I had no precise idea of the system of National Socialism. That is why I believed Fritz when he said: "That's how they all are." That Hitler's crime also consisted of forcing other people to go along with this system was something I grasped only later. I had become acquainted with "the Germans" in Lodz, in Auschwitz, on the marches, and in the camps. For me, Vienna was a city inhabited by Germans. Through Fritz I began to differentiate a bit. I saw that many soldiers had had to pay a price. They came to school on crutches, without legs and arms. I had only encountered those wearing German uniforms as Hitler's henchmen, as sadists and murderers. Fritz did not realize it, but he was the only one who could tell me about the suffering of the soldiers without offending me.

I wanted to know everything about this world that was completely unknown to me. Fritz explained how young people had been blinded by propaganda. That they had been shown films showing that Jews supposedly committed all sorts of heinous acts. This propaganda was so effective that the boys threw themselves with enthusiasm into often hopeless battles, ready to sacrifice their lives for the Führer. The photos that the Nazi propagandists had taken of us in Lodz came to mind.

Only now did I understand the insidiousness of their prejudice. I had to learn more about it. What could be done against it—how did it function, this poisoning of brains and hearts? How could this propaganda be defused? My vague hunger for knowledge was given a direction. Through a coincidence I heard of the existence of an institute of journalism. That's where I had to go.

My formal education had been interrupted after grammar school and only briefly and inadequately continued at Marysin. Actually the course of my education had been interrupted for five years. I didn't know anything, I couldn't do anything, but I wanted to know everything. It took me until 1949 to finish my Matura. Those who had fought in the war and the few of us concentration camp survivors were not made a gift of it, but it was made easier for us. It represented no more and no less than the right to study at a school of higher education. Nevertheless it demanded all of our energy, not because of the unfamiliar surroundings of the big city, but because of our continuing emotional problems and our still weakened health. For me, studying for the Matura was constantly interrupted by having to spend time in the hospital.

In 1949 I began studying journalism. People there were very nice to me. In a recent lecture, one of my teachers, Frau Dr. Marianne Lunzer, mentioned the young man from Poland who was always asking everyone everything. I must have gotten on their nerves considerably, because in my desire for knowledge I accosted everyone, pushed myself on everyone. There were many new, interesting acquaintances to make. The well-known news commentator Hugo Portisch was one of my fellow students as was the later editor-in-chief of the *Kronen Zeitung,* Friedrich "Bibi" Dragon.

Rysiek studied medicine. At home he plunged into not only his textbooks but also into the documents of the past. He studied the atrocities of the Nazis, wanting to know everything that happened. I didn't. I wanted to know what could happen, what should happen, what we could do about it. And although I read a lot, I sought the answers primarily in conversations, in encounters.

We both shared the feeling of guilt. It was absurd. The Nazis did not seem to feel guilty for what they had done, nor did the Viennese population seem to feel guilty for what they had allowed. In any case, one didn't notice any guilty feelings on their part. But we Jews felt guilty for being alive. This guilt had to be slowly reduced, there was a price to pay for it. In my case the price consisted of not only doing something for myself, but also for others. Of course no one acts altogether selflessly. With these deeds I wanted to justify my existence. A practical answer had to be given to the question of why I was alive.

During the lonely nights I reported back to my mother. In imaginary dialogues I told her proudly about survival but contradicted myself by trying to justify it. There was little to tell about money or career. I had no interest in money. My stipend was enough for me.

Among the numerous black-market dealers in Vienna, plenty were Jewish. For many it was necessary to trade care packages for money. How else could one eke out any kind of an existence completely alone and cut off from everything? Things were different among my non-Jewish acquaintances. A wealthy uncle or some relative always turned up at a wedding or some event who could make an apartment, some household goods, or some clothing available. The Jews were lacking family support or connections. Now and then there was a measure of understandable vindictiveness from people who had a bit more today than their tormentors of yesterday. I do not wish to be misunderstood, I condemned the black-market dealers as immoral. But what was morality in times of war and postwar? In any case, public resentment fell on Jews dealing on the black market, while among our circle of friends most people went hungry so that they could give parts of their care packages away to express or obtain affection.

I didn't want to get rich. Money was not my driving force. If I ended up studying a bit longer and started to practice my profession a bit later, it was all the same to me. I only wanted to learn. But learning alone was not enough. Working towards creating a community became just as important to me.

At the beginning of 1947, a few young people founded the Association of Jewish University Students (Vereinigung jüdischer Hochschüler or VJH). The primary task of this organization consisted of looking after six hundred students. They were impoverished, lonely, and plagued with emotional problems. They had no parents, little or no knowledge of the language of the country, and had not completed their education. Many were still battling illness and the effects of the concentration camps. For various reasons they had to complete their studies quickly.

Not all of them had come from the camps. Some had succeeded in hiding themselves. Many had fled from the East, from Poland, Hungary, Czechoslovakia, from Latvia, Lithuania, and Romania. In age, this group of six hundred was also in no way homogeneous. Next to twenty-year-olds sat thirty-five-year-olds and forty-year-olds to continue their interrupted studies.

All of these people thought primarily about themselves, about their future. Some only wanted to make money, so that they could finally start a family and make a new life for themselves. Many wanted simply to move forward and away from here, but first it was necessary just to survive the day. That necessitated not only food, but community as well. The six hundred students were seeking this community, but there had to be someone to organize it.

The founding chairman of the VJH was Alexander Guttmann. He came from Poland as well and was a few years older than me. My friend Frante Spitzer was among the founding members. Through him I was in close contact with the VJH from the beginning, and contributed to their activities even before I started to study in the University.

The goal I had set for myself, to justify my survival through social work, fortunately coincided with my talents. In Bad Goisern I had already been called "Chief" because I always volunteered when there was something to push through or organize. I had a talent for public speaking; it was never difficult for me to express myself when I listened to what my heart was saying.

We organized vacation camps at Semmering, where the Jewish sports club *Hakoah* had a cabin. We organized a camp for DP students in Reichenau-Edlach. Three hundred people came together there; the Joint supplied us with food, the Americans with cots. One problem was that Edlach was situated in the Russian Zone. I went to the Russian headquarters in Gloggnitz and looked for an officer. I told him that I was a Jew, and that I had been in a concentration camp; I was here now to ask for a transit pass for the food delivery from the Joint. He left me waiting there a moment, then returned with another officer, who spoke to me in Yiddish. Naturally I was given the transit pass.

At Semmering I organized a soccer match for *Hakoah* with the English and the Russians. Some wealthy ladies were staying in the hotel next to our summer camp. They took a collection among themselves to buy us butter and milk. Once a rich Jew whose daughter was celebrating her birthday invited all of us to the party. It seemed like a fairy tale because there was so much to eat.

From 1949 to 1953 along with Paul Grosz, now president of the Jewish Community, and Ruth Herzl, who was particularly dedicated, I was in charge of social affairs for the VJH. I was elected president of the VJH and served in this role from 1952 to 1959. Then I felt able to give my mother a proud report about what I had achieved.

Now I had a clear goal before me. My work for the Jews in Vienna was essentially for the youth of this community. It unavoidably brought me into conflict with the established Jewish Community. Superficially, the reasons for that were of a political nature. We Eastern European Jews had a Zionist orientation. The interests of Austro-German Jews focused on Vienna, and they were criticized generally for a lack of Jewish consciousness. We met with a different worldview when these so-called "Viennese Jews" came back from their exile. For the most part these people hadn't lived through 1938 in this city, because they had emigrated earlier.

The creation of the State of Israel gave us a feeling of security and self-confidence. In a certain way, our meaningless suffering was given a point of reference outside ourselves. The generation that had to suffer the *Shoah*, the Holocaust, received restitution with the establishment of our own Jewish state. We young people took the creation of Israel personally, without ever having been there.

It was a jubilant moment for us when, according to his explicit wish, the body of Theodor Herzl, the founder of Zionism, was exhumed from his grave in Döbling and brought to Israel. For the first time we saw an airplane of the State of Israel with its blue and white emblem, for the first time we saw young Israeli soldiers in uniform. The Jewish State was close enough to touch.

The presidency of the official Jewish Community had first been in the hands of the government-appointed (that is, by Ernst Fischer) Brill. This position—that is, the head of the Jewish Community—went over to the Social Democrats after the elections. The Cold War, which broke out in 1947, engendered various political positions, which could only remain incomprehensible to people with a background like ours. Among the six hundred students was a vast array of political convictions, from Communists to Social Democrats to Zionists.

We had very little energy left over for fighting a small-scale Cold War. Our first conflict with the official Jewish Community was because its leadership demanded that the VJH separate from its Communist wing. I was against this even before being elected president. "I will not participate in a selection of Jews," was my reasoning. The new president of the official Community, Emil Maurer, a Social Democrat who had returned from London, insinuated sweepingly that the Jewish students showed "pro-Communist" tendencies. This made me all the more angry because I myself was a confirmed Social Democrat.

One can hardly imagine two more different ways of seeing one and the same conflict. We Jewish students did not really have political interests. We were so busy that politics took only second place within our organization. The first goal still consisted of easing the difficulties of survival, strengthening our community morally and physically. We felt that we were the ones who had lived through something. Now the people returned who had gone into exile and wanted to take up where Austria had left off at the time, with political strife between the parties. But we were not interested in this strife. We wanted warmth and unity.

Naturally we were being unfair. The considerable organizational work of the Jewish Community in finding living quarters, clothing, and food, in refugee work and in negotiations with the authorities was something we took for granted. There were certainly people in the Community who understood us. Jakob Bindel, who was responsible for social affairs and organized the clothing distribution on Seitenstettengasse, was extremely sympathetic to us and often tried to arbitrate in this conflict.

Director Wilhelm Krell, a serious, intelligent man, had been in Auschwitz himself. He had lost his wife there; his small daughter, their only child, had died in his arms. He discussed many things with me, and sometimes I had the impression that he was in serious doubt as to whether we weren't right after all with our demands and our criticism. It was Krell who brought Simon Wiesenthal to Vienna from Linz and helped him in establishing the Jewish Historical Documentation Center. His Documentation Center for identifying Nazi war criminals expanded on work begun by Tuvia Friedman and Kurt Weigel in Vienna.

For the most part, these Viennese Jews were strangers to us; on the other hand, they probably saw us as strange concentration camp Jews from the East. There was also a difference in appearance. Emil Maurer, a former revolutionary socialist born in 1884, was portly and came to the Community office dressed in a Styrian hat and loden coat. Although many of the Viennese Jews liked us personally, in general they lacked the generosity and warmth that we expected. In the Jewish Community's offices, a former palace consisting of five floors on Schottenring, there was no room for the Jewish youth organizations to meet. Each official had a large, airy room to himself, but we were pushed away into the dark, shabby, unrenovated Seitenstettengasse.

We felt we had a right to everything. We wanted this building opened to us. We considered ourselves to be the Jewish community of tomorrow. They gave us nothing, not even a room for our activitities. Meanwhile, they complained that we danced "till the window panes shook" at our weekly meetings. Of course it was not mentioned that at these meetings we celebrated Jewish traditions together, listened to lectures, or watched films before we began dancing.

We criticized the "old guard" for selling off Jewish property to the township of Vienna. I was against the Jewish Community, with its common Social Democratic base, joining forces with the city administrators and selling our property too cheaply. Some of the present community housing in the second district is built on ground that was purchased much too inexpensively from the Jewish Community. Naturally, the bureaucrats in the Community were not pleased to hear my accusations that it was squandering our property.

We saw in this a gesture of self-surrender. How could a viable community evolve, when it went about giving away its reinstated property? This is why we opposed those policies and took the stand that Vienna should once again become a flourishing Jewish community. The socialist leadership of the official Community complained about me, the socialist, to the Socialist Party, and accusing me of acting against the Party. It turned into a case for arbitration. Otto Probst and Counselor Lachs sat in the Party's arbitration court. Lachs, who walked with crutches, swung one of the crutches in the air, pointed to me and cried indignantly: "If one more person complains about this young man, he's going to have to deal with me!" Whereupon the case was closed in my favor.

What angered people such as Maurer even more was my accusation that they didn't put any heart into their work. This accusation stung. It led to the founding of a newsletter by the Jewish university students. In 1951 I started it with my fellow students Rita Koch, Otto Kahn, Kurt Weigel, and Iszek Merdinger. We called it *Das Jüdische Echo* (The Jewish Echo). At the beginning it was financed entirely from donations. The constant theme of the paper could be summarized by the title of one of my articles: "Where There's No Heart." Written in 1955, it spoke out against the Community's policy: "Yes, the elderly and poor are taken care of, as far as the budget and the Joint contributions allow. But instead of doing things with enthusiasm and vigor, it is with routine and 'dignity of office' that things get done. Where the official's heart still breaks through—that happens, too, thank heavens—it is against the general atmosphere and also in spite of it."

As one can imagine, *The Jewish Echo* was a permanent annoyance to the Community. Maurer posed the question in the Social Democratic Jewish newspaper *Demokratischer Bund:* "Is it not a waste of money printing a paper that is of no political or literary use?" Reference was made to a certain Zelman, who was "Führer" of the Jewish university students. Maurer urged them to get him.

They wouldn't even consider it. On the contrary, they were unanimously behind me. The Jewish youth had its own vision of the future of the Jewish community in Vienna and *The Jewish Echo* became its rallying point. One who supported us without reservation was the community elder Elias Shapira, a lumber merchant. He and other Jewish citizens made it possible through their contributions for *The Jewish Echo* to rise from its origins as a newsletter into a respectable and, later, an internationally renowned cultural magazine.

In truth, the Jewish community didn't have much to do with its leadership. The true Jewish community arose in the years directly following the end of the war. Due to the city's geopolitical situation some Jews remained in Vienna because they could not go further, because they didn't want to go further, or because they, like myself, had been misplaced here. Of the approximately seven hundred Jews who were still in Vienna by 1945—that is, those who had intermarried or had otherwise gone underground—very few decided to remain; still fewer survivors originally from Vienna had come back. It was not the Viennese Jews but poor and sick concentration camp survivors and people who had fled from the East who made up the core of the postwar Viennese Jewish community.

This group was only marginally interested in Austrian politics. Rising anti-Semitism could not be overlooked. I remember taking part in demonstrations against a Rommel film at the beginning of the fifties. Still, we were less upset by these public manifestations than by the private ones such as I had experienced at Erika's and which each of us experienced in some form. Those who had lived through the year 1938 in Vienna made sure that they left. They said to us: "You don't know the Austrians." Nevertheless, it was just this generalization that I refused to accept.

We were aware of how the Austrian political parties courted the votes of the old Nazis, but we let ourselves be pacified. We wanted to trust the words of people like Leopold Figl and Oskar Helmer when they came to speak at our commemoration ceremonies. At the time, we didn't know that they were doing everything they could to thwart the resolution of the question of restitution. That they lied to us and deceived us, that they had resolved not to invite Jewish Austrians to return to Austria, we had no idea. We did notice that they shifted the blame for the war and destruction onto Germany, and that they used the excuse that Austria had been a victim of Hitler to deny any responsibility.

On the other hand, we were grateful that six hundred Jewish students had the chance to finish their Matura examinations quickly and study in Austria. Our gratitude for that and our hopes for rebuilding a Jewish world after Hitler prevented deep thinking about the Nazi past and the present. Yet we were not ignorant. We felt more than we knew about the government's attitude. Perhaps we pushed this feeling aside in order to live here. For this reason we did not concern ourselves very deeply with Austrian politics; the future of Israel seemed more important to us than the future of Vienna.

Possibly this explains our rage against the policy of the official Jewish Community: It seemed senseless for us to demand that the Austrians understand us—but we demanded it of the Jews. We demanded that they recognize our reconstruction work for what it was: the overcoming of the Hitler years through practical life. I couldn't understand why the Community didn't want to give everything it could to its youth, open all its doors, make everything available to it. We did not get what we demanded until much later and by that time, the original six hundred students of VJH had long since scattered to the four winds.

Perhaps I demanded too much from the leadership of the Community. It was busy organizing life, regulating housing and administrative questions, setting up homes for returning Viennese Jews. They knew little about our years of self-help and reconstruction, how we struggled to make a life in the language of our tormentors, how hungry we were for any kind of community. They knew nothing about how my own search for community took me one step further, because I felt that my survival required more of me than just a secure existence. Little did they know that our hunger for community had to do with literal hunger. Although the kitchen of the American Joint supplied our meals and gave us food, often we suffered from empty stomachs. Rather than getting into illicit trade, I went up and down Kärntner Strasse trying to find a wealthy acquaintance who could be drawn into conversation and perhaps invite me out to eat.

Restless and meddlesome as I was, I soon found out that these meals could be organized. As with the poor on *erev shabbes* in the shtetl, we DP students were now invited to dinner on Friday evenings. I distributed the host addresses and impressed on the invitees that they should be grateful in any case and declare the food wonderful, even if it wasn't that good. After all, we wanted to keep getting invited!

Unfortunately, one young person did not follow these rules completely. Two days later I received a phone call from the hostess: "My dear Leon Zelman, don't send me any fresh boys again!" She was beside herself, but she didn't tell me what had happened. I took the young man to task.

"What did you do?"

"Well, she asked me how the fish tasted. I said that my mother's was better."

I was furious. This fellow did not come from a concentration camp; he had come to Vienna to study and didn't appreciate what he was offered.

"You won't be getting anymore chances," I said to him. And that's what happened.

We did it not only for food, but to have contact with families. All of us were alone. For years we lived only with our memories. These Jewish families opened their homes to us, although many of them were still living out of suitcases themselves, not sure how long they would stay here. Incidentally, most of them did stay. Living in Vienna today are numerous Jewish doctors, engineers, and lawyers who are the sons and daughters of those Eastern Jews living out of their suitcases after the war.

Their names summon up feelings of thankfulness and homecoming in me, together with the pleasant memory of feeling full. There were the Blodingers in the third district, the Schragers, the Laufs, the Rosen-kranzes on Mariahilfer Strasse, the Mandelbaums on Taubstummengasse, the Landaus. There was double pleasure at the Gleichers: She was a fabulous cook, he understood how to convey to us the meaning of the Jewish holidays in a cogent and modern way. In some homes there was an elegant atmosphere, almost a drawing-room refinement, while in others the feeling was more earthy and substantial, like in the shtetl. In some of them there was the familiar smell of *shabbes*, of gefilte fish and chicken, in the stairwell.

We fell upon these "*Yiddishe mammes*" who took us in like sons, and stuffed us until we couldn't hold anymore. The fathers were wonderful—understanding and cultivated men. These Sabbaths, these holidays, be-came a substitute for my shtetl. I was actually accused of wanting to make a shtetl out of the Viennese Jewish community. Yes, that is just what I wanted to do. I wanted to create a community. I organized these dinner invitations, I impressed upon my fellow students how they had to behave, and I took on the reprimands when something went wrong. I took over, so to speak, the role of a secularized *shammes* who placed the *shabbes* guests. We went to the synagogue only on the High Holy Days, Rosh Hashanah and Yom Kippur. Most of us had turned away from religion. The thought of how God could have allowed all that to happen embittered us. But we went to synagogue on these holidays and *yahrzeits*. We valued the synagogue as a social institution. The rabbi spoke to us with very compassinate words. We cried together. Anything was better than to be alone with one's memories.

One Jewish house stood out from the rest, that of the Pollacks. Counselor Pollack was the head doctor of the Vienna police. He was married to a non-Jewish woman who had followed her children voluntar-ily to the concentration camp Theresienstadt; he himself had survived Auschwitz. On the High Holy Days he appeared in his impressive uni-form, decorated with all of his medals and an oversized uniform hat. At his side he wore an enormous sabre. He always gave me the impression of being an impersonator, even though the uniform was real. Perhaps that impression came from the fact that he wore built-up shoes in order to appear taller than his height of five feet five inches. His kindly face contrasted in the strangest way with his martial appearance. These Pollacks were touchingly concerned about us single students. Their huge apartment on Porzellangasse was always open to us. They had even set up chess tables for us.

How could we show all these people our gratitude? The Jewish university students organized a ball. We were audacious enough to call it *bal paré*. I still don't know today what that means exactly, but it sounded very elegant. I don't remember anymore whose idea it was, but it was a good one. We wanted to do something nice for the older people who had come to Vienna from the concentration camps, from the DP camps, from hiding places in the woods. The halls of the Messepalast, where it was held, were festively decorated. Fritz Muliar was hired to recite, Maxi Böhm played the master of ceremonies for a bowl of soup. Herbert Reisner and Hanka Weigel organized the program; the women baked and cooked for the buffet for days before, and dance master Elmayer choreographed the polonaise.

Now that was really a polonaise, with all the young and old Poles, Hungarians, Romanians, and Czechs in our costumes and suits from Lambert Hofer's costume rental. In truth the event was more like a ghostly masquerade. But the old people cried for joy that after all they had been through, they could still experience something like this. They admired each other and their children in their rented tuxedos and evening clothes. There was a wild confusion of styles; brand-new jewelry sparkled against faded lace. Tears of joy flowed after all that suffering. The fake glamour gave these people a moment of dignity. They came up to me and embraced me. "Thank you Leon, that was so beautiful," they said.

Through such encouragement and recognition I gradually found my place. Each success of Jewishness in this city was part of my success over Hitler. He wanted a city free of Jews. I wanted a proud, self-confident, and humane Jewish community, not a group of groveling conformists, indulged moral cowards, and stubborn bureaucrats. Today I can say: I was looking for an excuse to stay here.

In 1947 a letter reached me that put me into a state of tremendous excitement. Finally, finally I received news from one of my relatives. My cousin Hanka, whom I had long since believed to be dead, wrote to me from Sweden. She had found out my address from the Red Cross and did everything she could to obtain a visa for me to visit her. At Christmastime 1947, I took a train for Helsingborg. What a contrast to Vienna! Nothing gloomy—no ruins, no rubble, no hunger. The city was peaceful and clean in the snow. Hanka was married and lived with her husband Jack in a Jewish neighborhood with colorful houses full of children.

The joy over this reunion in this idyllic place—the warmth, the tranquility, the apparent well-being, the acceptance as a member of this family—overwhelmed me. I stuffed myself so full of all the rich dishes that I damaged my liver and had to spend two weeks in the hospital. The care in the hospital, and the visits from relatives and acquaintances, made it almost nicer than staying at Hanka's. I lay quietly and listened to the church bells ringing. I wished this hospital stay would last forever.

Equipped with four suitcases full of shoes, clothing, and food I went back to Vienna. Hanka and Jack accompanied me as far as Copenhagen and went shopping with me there. From the time of this visit, they have been like sister and brother to me. It was a good feeling, not to be alone in the world.

I had hardly set foot in Vienna again when I was seized by my old doubts. Why was I alive, why not my brother, my father and my mother? Despite all of my work for the community, I could not get over what I had experienced. I discussed it frequently with Rysiek, but we couldn't really help each other. Our problems were too similar. When we tried to talk about it we only tore open wounds. Rysiek became bitter and sought answers in his history books. I clung to the consciousness that there were a few hundred young people who needed me. I told myself that they were my family, I had to do something for them to justify my survival.

We lacked any kind of psychological care. One of the DP's ran around for years with a piece of bread and a roll of toilet paper in his pocket. Some married hastily to escape their loneliness. My depressions sometimes led to apathy, which made it hard for me to study. Putting off examinations, on the other hand, drove me to despair. In addition, there was my tuberculosis, with its attacks of fever and sweating. Due to years of subordinating ourselves to orders that had to be followed or else face death, our will was not particularly pronounced. There was a temptation to let oneself go; suicide was a solution that seemed to suggest itself. It was chosen by many in our surroundings. Even I thought more than once about this way out.

I was lucky. The Joint arranged for me to see the lung specialist Professor Felix Mlczoch, a doctor who was not suspected of having any anti-Semitic or National Socialist tendencies. He was the son-in-law of Friedrich Funder, the former publisher of the monarchist *Reichspost* and later publisher of *Die Furche*. Mlczoch looked after me. I brought him my medical records from Bad Goisern. He got in touch with the camp doctor. When I did not appear for therapy because I lay at home depressed, he called me up and scolded me. Then he encouraged me: "Come on, get up, carry on, you can make it." Get up, carry on. I seemed to need these orders, because I got up and went on.

Once, when I let myself sink in a particularly weak moment, he slapped my face. "Get a hold of yourself!" he shouted at me. At the beginning I still went to the commemoration ceremonies at Mauthausen and Ebensee. Mlczoch forbade me to go. He advised me not to seek these confrontations. But he encouraged me to continue my inner dialogue with my mother, to report my success in my studies to her. He helped me. He was everything to me.

He took me home with him. I could go to his office at Otto-Wagner-Platz whenever I wanted. If I slept poorly, I went to see him. Sometimes I sat for hours in his waiting room. When I reported that I couldn't sleep he explained, "You have two parts in your body. Your head is confused, but your heart is good." He assured me that I was intelligent and clever. I owed it to my father, my mother, and my brother to advance myself. He took a lot of time with me. When I started to smoke, he dragged me into his X-ray room and showed me pictures of how my lungs would look.

He treated me for almost ten years. Once I collapsed in his office after having had a horrible nightmare. Often he didn't know how to react, but resolved to play the role of a stern father. I never resented him for once slapping my face because his intentions were good. He talked to me later about it: this was not an apology, but an explanation of his behavior.

Through Dr. Mlczoch I was drawn into the circle around Friedrich Funder and *Die Furche*, which was then an important Catholic weekly newspaper. Its writers represented the best of what Catholicism had to offer in Vienna at the time. I didn't know that they were considered progressive Catholics. It wouldn't have mattered to me. I was fascinated by their intellectuality. They took me in, although I was just as ignorant as I was curious.

There I became acquainted with the historian Friedrich Heer. He invited me to his home. With his breathless, expansive way of speaking he seemed like a saint to me. I was deeply impressed with the huge library in his apartment in the fourth district. From him I first learned the historical background of Judaism. He gave me the feeling that I was important because I was a Jew. He explained his theory of National Socialism to me, why the Nazis wanted to wipe out Judaism as well as

Jews. It was because they were anti-Christian, he claimed, and argued that the dialogue between Jews, Christians, and their enemies must continue. His successful book *Dialog der Feinde* (*Dialogue of Enemies*) had just been published.

I took my examination for philosophy with the sociologist August Maria Knoll. He invited me home to his tiny apartment in the fifteenth district; it had no running water. I helped him carry water in from the hall, so I wouldn't have to miss even an instant of his presence. Knoll, too, explained to me what Christian civilization owed to Judaism. In contrast to Heer, who almost swallowed his words, Knoll spoke slowly, with an exquisite vocabulary. Only now did it become clear to me what we Jews had given the world. Like Heer, he spoke of the achievements of the famous Viennese Jews. He mentioned all the renowned names from Gustav Mahler to Sigmund Freud, Arthur Schnitzler, and Arnold Schönberg.

Through Heer and Knoll I began to appreciate the place where I had landed. Now an interest in Judaism on an intellectual level began to awake in me. I loved these men for giving me this knowledge. One of the places in which the Jewish people had amassed their most notable achievements was Vienna. I was in Vienna. Wonderful! When I listened to these upright Christians I almost believed that Vienna was the center of the Jewish world!

I began to read up on all of this. And I began to draw confidence from what Heer told me; it was because the Nazis perceived the Jews to be such a powerful intellectual enemy that they sought to annihilate them with such vehemence. He cited the Jewish philosophers, he spoke of Martin Buber, of the Marxists and explained that the Austrian constitution, one of the best in the world, had been written by Hans Kelsen, a Jew. He lent me books written by these people, called me "my dear boy" (although he was only twelve years older than I), and with his arm around my shoulder and talking the entire time, he walked with me through the fourth district, up Favoritenstrasse, past the Theresianum and over to Belvedere, where there was a good view of Vienna.

My simple idea of establishing a home based on community and a Jewish family was now enriched by the intellectual background of Judaism. The existence of Israel as a state and the presence of the Americans in Vienna assured us a secure existence. My studies in journalism gave me prospects for earning a living. The task I had given myself of looking after the six hundred students provided me with a purpose. All that was missing was a perspective.

Once a week I went to the hospital for a check-up on my lung disease. Coincidentally, I became acquainted with Peter Strasser there. I can't remember the exact circumstances of this meeting, but I remember my immediate fascination with him. Strasser, who was eleven years older than I, had fled from the Nazis to France, had fallen prey to them there, but had been able to escape. In 1945 he was elected to the executive committee of the Austrian Socialist Party, the SPÖ; he was also named chairman of the Socialist Youth of Austria and chairman of Youth International. From 1949 on, he was a member of parliament, and from 1950, a member of the European Council.

Strasser was one of the foremost political figures of the Second Republic. In his memoirs Bruno Kreisky called him "one of the most talented young leaders of the Social Democrats." He died early and tragically of leukemia in 1962. Peter Strasser took me to his home on Währingerstrasse in the eighteenth district, where his apartment was open to politically-minded young people. There I became acquainted with people like Otto Probst, Heinz Nittel, Karl Czernetz, later Heinz Fischer and Leopold Gratz.

Probst had been General Secretary of the SPÖ since 1946. As a former inmate of the Buchenwald concentration camp, he took a special interest in me. Nittel was the youngest in this circle. He was two years younger than I and fascinated by Israel; later he became president of the

Austro-Israeli Society. His love for Israel probably cost him his life, because in 1981 he was the victim of an assassination by Palestinians in Vienna. Leopold Gratz impressed me as one of the most intelligent in this circle. As parliamentary secretary he did his best to facilitate contact with Israel. An enduring friendship arose between us which has lasted to this day.

We sat together, many times all night, discussing many subjects and singing songs. For the first time I had found a sense of community that was outside my own circle. That gave me hope, hope for another world. For it was still the search for a home, for security, for a substitute family that drove me on. I admit it, I pushed myself on everyone to get a little love.

Now I sat with many obviously like-minded people, to whom my being here, my Jewishness, did not matter, on the floor of Strasser's apartment and listened to proposals for a new world. Karl Czernetz had returned from exile in London in spirit against a coalition with the ÖVP, the Austrian People's Party, although he felt it was necessary. I understood German much better now, but still not well enough. Not every little detail of what was said, however, mattered to me. Here was the radical split with the Nazi past, here was a future, here was a new world. I was, inspired. Here was my new home. Peter Strasser took me by the shoulders, looked me in the eyes and said: "Leon, you are going to have a beautiful world." Of course I became a member of the Socialist Party.

I had reached my goal of trying to make Vienna into a kind of shtetl. The six hundred fellow students and the old Jews from the East were my family. The Catholic thinkers took the place of my philosophical Uncle Yankel, who explained the world to me, and the Joint, with its care packages, replaced Aunt Ruchele's dumplings. Now I had also found the visionaries who dreamed of a better future like the shtetl youth who met at the fountain and in the woods.

I moved freely among all of these worlds, went from one to the other. The young socialists showed me the future. They embraced the world. They were internationally oriented, they believed in a Europe-minded community. Strasser was a member of the European Council, Czernetz a member of the European Parliament. They spoke out against conservatism, even in their own party, but fought for tying Austria to the West, for a social democratic Europe.

Now I could join in the talk. At night, I told my mother about this world. I loved these people. I loved their songs. Here I found the warmth and enthusiasm that I had missed so much in the leadership of the Jewish Community. I went to every meeting. On the first of May, I stood in the bleachers at city hall where we sang "Brothers, to the sun, to freedom!" and *The Internationale*. I sang with enthusiasm. Vienna now offered me a future, studies, work, friends. My decision was firm: I would stay in this city.

Only one thing could have torn me away, perhaps. I still had Lusia on my mind, the girl who had appeared at Marysin and whom I had taken care of like a sister. Lusia had found my address and written to me. A childishly hopeful correspondence began. I lost myself in daydreams that followed the pattern of the noble knight: "I will come and rescue you." Before this could happen, I wanted to be something in life other than a poor student with a small stipend.

Before I concluded my studies, Lusia moved to New York to live with an aunt. The correspondence broke off. As soon as I had my degree I felt armed to face Lusia. I flew to New York, got help from a Jewish policeman in finding her address, and phoned her. "Leave her alone!" the aunt snapped on the telephone. I didn't let it stop me. Lusia's little daughter opened the door to my knock. Of course Lusia was married, of course our hearts did not meet. Thus Leon the Conquerer's dream turned out to be a castle in the air. I returned to Vienna.

Although I had earned my degree in 1954, I remained president of the Association of Jewish University Students until 1959. Only after the last of the six hundred had finished their studies and had scattered in all directions could I step down from my position in good conscience. Now I had to decide on a profession. In 1951–52 as president of VJH, I had been invited to visit Israel. We Jewish students had a special relationship to Israel: we believed that Israel's struggle had to be supported in the interest of the Jewish people.

In Israel, even then, I recognized tourism as an important means to this end. Through my studies I had come to the firm conviction that the Nazis' attempt to annihilate the Jews was possible only because of extensive and widespread ignorance of Jews and Judaism. It is difficult to hate people whom one knows. My main interest however consisted of making it possible for Jews to see and experience the State of Israel.

Thus, after concluding my studies I approached the Österreichisches Verkehrsbüro, the Austrian Travel Agency, with a proposal for building up tourism to Israel. They liked my idea. I got the job and soon sat in an office in their building on Landstrasser Hauptstrasse. It was a slow start, but it was a start.

Eventually the Israeli airline El Al did not want to keep its office at Stephansplatz any longer, because all the other airlines were moving their offices to the Ringstrasse. Coincidentally, around the same time Probst and Nittel asked me: "Leon, what can we do for you?" Most likely they were thinking of a position in an embassy or a cultural institute. I answered that I was already at home here in Vienna. I wanted to stay. But I had a fantastic idea. I suggested making Stephansplatz into a meeting place and running the El Al office as a branch of the Austrian Travel Agency. I would set up this branch mainly with an emphasis on Israel and make it available to the Jewish public.

In 1963 the agency opened a branch called the Reisebüro City, the City Travel Agency, under my direction at 10 Stephansplatz, in the heart of Vienna.

Full of pride I reported it to my mother. We three friends had come a long way. Frante lived in Switzerland representing major American publishing companies; Rysiek was a doctor in Vienna. I now had a task that corresponded to my aspirations. I was bursting with happiness and zest for life. I wanted to organize a community. And I wanted to reconcile the Jews with a Vienna that had become my home, a city that had conquered the shadows of its past.

CHAPTER FIVE

Making Vienna Home

I felt good in my new world. I stood on the bleachers at the May Day celebrations, where I had gone with my new friends. Below me was a sea of red flags as the socialist youth marched by, singing songs of brotherhood, the future, and their faith in the new world. I cried for joy, blinded by my tears.

I didn't see Austria's defects, because I didn't want to see them. My private act of repression, so that I could live and function, coincided with acts of official repression on the part of the Second Republic in an absurd way. The mood in the country had been against us from the start. When it showed itself and invited open opposition we stepped forward to meet it. We did not feel threatened by the anti-Semitic demonstrations in the DP camps directed openly against us since we knew that we would be protected by the Americans. But where this mood remained hidden, elusive, and quiescent, I did not try to analyze it. I did not make a connection between the obvious anti-Semitism and the anti-Semitism that quietly permeated the entire society. My refusal to accept this insight was an act of self-defense. I wanted to live here, and I had to be able to live here.

I had no idea of the extent to which this atmosphere existed and to what extent even those who addressed us with noble words on commemoration days were infected by anti-Semitism. That much of postwar politics in Austria was tactically motivated did not occur to me. That Austria described itself as Nazi Germany's first victim so that it would evade blame—which would have had political and material consequences—escaped me completely. The question of reparation did not interest me at the time because it did not represent a topic relevant to my existence. We had enough to do in concentrating on ourselves. In addition, Austria had succeeded in passing on the question of blame to the Federal Republic of Germany as the legal successor of the Third Reich. However, Germany's Konrad Adenauer had settled the question in 1952, while in the words of Interior Minister Oskar Helmer, Austria planned "to drag out the matter," which is what happened. To this day "the matter" has not been conclusively resolved.

Possibly I was happy to be talked into believing Austria's role as a victim. It made it easier for me to imagine living here, which was something that I was managing to do. Yet it required a certain amount of talent for repressing things. It was no different for the Austrian state. In my case, however, it was not necessary to tell lies for the sake of my existence.

I had no desire to look into the blackest depths. I wanted to look forward. How was I to know that the university now lacked people like Karl Popper or Richard von Mises, Karl Menger or Ludwig Wittgenstein? Or that by 1948, of four hundred emigrants who were willing to return to the University only seven had been brought back? How could I have grasped that the self-inflicted impoverishment of cultural life was voluntary and there was not really any interest in having one of the famous Jews come back? How could I have recognized in its full scope the shamelessly quick de-Nazification, as in the reinstatement of all the conductors, professors, and actors who were incriminated by their deeds in the Third Reich?

I didn't look very closely and yet the signs were everywhere. The same Minister Kolb who was a member of the festival committee of a

Hakoah celebration had publicly described the Republic of Austria in 1946 as the "first rightful claimant" of the restitution laws because "the major part of the wealth withdrawn [by the Nazis] was not withdrawn due to racist reasons but for political reasons." If I had known about Figl's statement that "the Jews just want to become rich quickly," how could I have tolerated his presence on the occasion of our Jewish commemoration days?

There were anti-Semitic remarks from all quarters of the government. A memorandum by the State Chancellery for Foreign Affairs in 1945 stated: "There is no Jewish state. Nevertheless, Jews play a major role in the world's foreign policy, on the one hand because a large part of the press is in their hands . . . and on the other because . . . the international finance capital is largely in Jewish hands." Foreign Minister Karl Gruber charged that: "The relevant writings of the World Jewish Congress are presented in a spiteful tone and bluntly demand that Austria should be held responsible for its participation in the war."

The whole panorama of Austrian anti-Semitism would have been laid out before me if I hadn't blinded myself with trust. In 1947, Mayor Theodor Körner published an impassioned denial of Viennese anti-Semitism in the *Wiener Zeitung:* "The originators of such untrue stories are known to us. They can be described as the worst well-poisoners and are on the brink of slandering their home country. Once and for all let it be said that besides the disturbances organized by the Nazis during the time of their power over Austria, Jewish pogroms never took place in Vienna because the Viennese are cosmopolitans and thus at the outset are not anti-Semites." Ironically, the language seemed to support precisely what he was refuting.

The modernity of the language and motives is amazing. In the case of Kurt Waldheim, the same language returned. Or had it ever disappeared? Conservatives and socialists, all of them followed the same tactics. Pretty speeches were given denying that anti-Semitism existed, or had ever existed, but in cabinet and government meetings, the idea was to drag out the matter. Even people like Bruno Kreisky and Karl Czernetz were not received with enthusiasm everywhere in their own party upon their return. Supposedly, Helmer only referred to Kreisky as "our Jew."

Much of this I couldn't know. I was ready to push aside some of it, to consider it a transitory sign of the times, the remains of a past that had been pushed aside by a new generation in a new state, just as the postwar rubble had been pushed off the streets. After the years in the ghetto and the camps I simply had no desire to feel cut off and demoralized again. I had to struggle with myself. I lived in a city in which I could identify every second or third young person as the enemy. How could I have coped with seeing many of those whom I wished for my allies as the very opposite?

And there was a further aspect: I had not spent 1938 in Vienna. I had not experienced how the Viennese had humiliated their Jewish fellow citizens, how they had robbed and stolen from them. Later, when through my activities I traveled abroad to visit Viennese emigrants all over the world, and these former Viennese told me what they had experienced in 1938, I understood how deep their estrangement went. If I had experienced all of that, I imagine I wouldn't have returned either. From one day to the next, a friend was no longer a friend, the janitor was a spy, the owner of the grocery shop an SS man. They remembered a Vienna filled with jubilation over Hitler, they remembered torturers and grinning onlookers.

Added to the humiliations and deprivations they had suffered, in 1945 there came a second humiliation and deprivation. No one encouraged the refugees to return. Quite the opposite. The state and political parties arranged things quickly with old Nazis. In several scandalous court verdicts, concentration camp contractors, Gestapo department heads, men who had leading roles in the mass murder of the Jews were either acquitted or given ridiculously minor sentences. After the midseventies Nazi criminals were no longer prosecuted by law. Through the "Amnesty for Minor Incriminations Act of 1948" many Nazis got back their property and were reinstated in high positions, while in the case of the Jews, the "victim" Austria shrank from reimbursing what had been stolen from them as long as it could. The Jews only care about money, it was said. From my experience I can say with certainty that it wasn't the money, it was the principle. In reality it was not the Jews, but the Austrian state that cared about money.

Moreover, the state actively concerned itself with integrating the old Nazis. In Austria alone the NSDAP had over half a million members, while the number of Viennese Jews at the end of 1948 did not exceed ten thousand. The government clearly understood the facts. "What was taken away from the Jews cannot be blamed on the 'Greater German Reich,'" conceded Interior Minister Helmer. "A major part went to our dear fellow citizens." However, he continued in the same breath, "I see the Jews spreading out everywhere, in trade especially in Vienna. Everything was taken away from the Nazis, too, in 1945, and we now see cases where even an educated National Socialist has to do construction work." Such open language was expressed only in closed cabinet meetings; the minutes were not publicized until the eighties. The atmosphere was so thick it could be felt, but still I did not grasp it.

Another development fueled my optimism—our euphoria over Israel. Since the founding of the State of Israel in 1948 it was clear to all Jews, even those without a Zionist orientation, that here was a piece of earth where they would be safe from persecution. Israel was truly a reference point for the confidence with which we tried to face the future.

On the other hand, the cynics in the Austrian government spoke about "atrocities of the Jews in Palestine," which would diminish the Jews' international reputation and would make it easier for the Austrian government to drag out the matter of reparations. Polls taken around the time that Israel was founded showed that approximately fifty percent of all Viennese held National Socialism to be a good cause that had only been badly applied. They believed in the old world, while we struggled for a new one. The openly anti-Semitic appearance of the neo-

Nazis supported my belief, because they provoked reactions. When we organized demonstrations against them, sometimes consisting of only two hundred people, sometimes of over a thousand, we gave each other confidence. I went into the street with my young socialist friends, with Catholics and Communists, to protest against desecrating cemeteries, swastika graffiti, and nationalistic festivities; we demonstrated against films that glorified National Socialist philosophy; we fought against the brazen neo-fascist organizations.

The climax of these conflicts was represented by the Borodajkewicz affair. Taras Borodajkewicz was one of those incorrigible professors who flaunted their anti-Semitic and neo-Nazi convictions, thereby gaining the approval of the RFS (right-wing) students. Although he had been a member of the Nazi Party in the thirties, when it was illegal, he was readmitted as a university professor in 1955 and gave lectures at the Hochschule für Welthandel (School of International Trade). The socialist students had been running an open campaign against him since 1962, which resulted in nothing more than a parliamentary inquiry without consequences.

In 1965, at a televised press conference, Borodajkewicz got carried away and made anti-Semitic remarks and statements about Israel, evoking derisive laughter from his right-wing radical audience. After this, there were two large demonstrations. One of the protagonists in the fight against Borodajkewicz was Ferdinand Lacina, who had prepared transcripts of Borodajkewicz's lectures. Now Lacina walked in the first row of a crowd of thousands of demonstrators in a march organized by the Austrian Resistance Movement. I marched beside him with my friends, among them Heinz Nittel, Peter Schieder, Leopold Gratz, and Erwin Lanc. I did not know Lacina, but I was full of pride that the city in which I lived brought forth such young men.

The neo-Nazis who attacked us and yelled "Heil Auschwitz" seemed like depraved and cowardly creatures. After each attack they turned and ran away. The Nazis were scared of us; I felt that a future was walking along beside me that I could rely on. When I heard Lacina speak at the demonstration I had the confirmation I needed to stay here. Here was logic, talent, enthusiasm, dedication. These people wouldn't let us down. I was also a speaker. I had no fear, but the Nazis were afraid. The scenes of the street fights and speeches felt like a second liberation to me. The old system was on the defensive.

At this demonstration one of the Nazis killed a demonstrator, a Communist named Ernst Kirchweger. Subsequently, at the funeral almost twenty thousand people came to show their solidarity with the victim including many important politicians from the SPÖ and ÖVP. Despite the tragic occasion, the Borodajkewicz affair was a victory for us.

Borodajkewicz had to go. Not until a year later, and with all the benefits due him, but nevertheless he went. A precedent had been set and I took strength from it. This is a new Vienna, this is a new generation, I told myself. This was the city that I wished to represent abroad, this was my home. For years I gave accounts of this new Vienna abroad, at a time when outside Austria it was still a widely held belief that all Austrians were Nazis. Simon Wiesenthal reproached me for this. I conceded him the right to make these reproaches, as his life's work consists of tracing war criminals. Yet I believed that if a viable Jewish community was to exist in Vienna, it had to have lively relations abroad, which meant at least Israel and other places where former Viennese Jews lived. To make Vienna a Jewish metropolis again was an unattainable goal, but it was possible to establish a vital Jewish community in Vienna. Toward this goal, I did not shy away from selling Vienna. The reactions to the agitator Borodajkewicz and the existence of young people like Lacina confirmed that I was right. Thus Lacina became part of my story, although I did not know him personally.

After this episode, my optimism soared. At the time Heinz Nittel was the Vienna City Councillor responsible for transport, which included tourism. He was particularly attached to Israel, and one day he had the idea of establishing the Jewish Welcome Service. More than a quarter of a century had passed since the end of the war. Many Jews who had thought they would never return to Vienna now thought about it, at least to visit family graves. There was need for an official post to look after these people. And Vienna needed the right person to care for these special guests.

The place was correctly chosen, and apparently the person as well. I threw myself into my new task. Stone from Israel was used to decorate a small room at the City Travel Agency, bringing an aura of Jerusalem, an impression of the Western Wall, to Stephansplatz.

The Jewish Welcome Service was opened in 1978. Chief Rabbi Akiva Eisenberg, father of the present Chief Rabbi, dedicated the new rooms. Leopold Gratz, my old friend from the days of the Strasser circle, was the mayor of Vienna at the time and awarded me the city's Silver Medal of Honor. I have received numerous official honors, but this is one of my favorites. Jakob Bindel, whom we had appreciated so much for his warmth and kindness during the disputes between Jewish students and the Community, also gave a speech in my honor.

I now had an area twice as big to realize my dreams: the travel agency and the Jewish Welcome Service. Added to that was a third, intellectual domain. With the disintegration of our student community of six hundred The Jewish Echo had lost its function as an internal newsletter. I had resigned as president of the Jewish students in 1959 but continued to publish The Jewish Echo as editor-in-chief, now on behalf of the Jewish students and alumni.

I planned to make a cultural periodical out of the The Jewish Echo which would be unique in the German-speaking world, a journal in which young Austrian intellectuals could express themselves, whether or not they were Jewish. At the demonstrations against Borodajkewicz I realized that a large number of non-Jews were on our side. Friedrich Heer and the young socialists had shown me the necessity of promoting interfaith dialogue.

Thus *The Jewish Echo* developed into a kind of drawing room forum where the best of Austrian intellectual life could find themselves besides internationally renowned thinkers. Besides, I placed great value on giving young and unknown intellectuals the chance to publish their work. It would be impossible to list the names of all the contributors. Let it suffice to say that only a few of the best were missing. The issues had an annual theme and were sent all over the world.

The implicit message was that work like this too could come forth from Vienna, thinkers of this caliber could publish here. The contributors ranged from Nahum Goldmann to Jean-Paul Sartre, from Isaac Bashevis Singer to Manès Sperber, from Murray G. Hall to Claudio Magris. *The Jewish Echo,* my Viennese drawing room, resounded with their voices.

I intended to give the *Echo* more tasks than a conventional cultural magazine. It was to serve young people as an educational program, giving them information about the history and traditions of Jewish life in Vienna. This information is more accessible today, but at that time it was dispersed and could not be found so easily. Meanwhile, the address list of the *Echo* also continued the invisible network of the six hundred. For them, the *Echo* was a tie to a place that perhaps only from a distance felt like home: Vienna. The *Echo* was like a piece of homeland, sent annually.

The least conspicuous purpose of the *Echo* was to satisfy my own curiosity, my own yearning for knowledge about Jewish subjects in general and about Jewish life in Austria in particular. My thirst for knowledge led me from subject to subject. I developed into something of a broker of ideas.

It was the youth who were always my highest priority. I had not given up on the old people but the youth were dear to my heart: the young Jews who often left the city to pursue their careers out in the world, the young Christians and socialists, born after the war, who were trying to build up a new Austria. I felt I had something to share with them.

Thus I declared my readiness to go into the schools and make myself available as a historical witness. Fred Sinowatz, the Minister of Education, and Kurt Scholz, the President of the Vienna Board of Education, initiated an information campaign on contemporary history. Peter Dusek from ORF, Austrian Radio and Television, accompanied me and recorded the talks for radio. Young people brought Nazi literature to me at school and asked me about stories they had been told by their grandparents, in which Hitler often came across much better than he did in accounts from their teachers.

Once we organized a visit to Israel for a Viennese Catholic school. The students were affected by many discoveries. First there was the visit to the Holocaust museum, Yad Vashem, which gave the children something to think about. But there were others as well. For example, when we visited a kibbutz I saw some of them put their heads together, puzzled about something. When I asked them it turned out that they were curious about the sight of a blond tractor driver. Was there such a thing as a blond Jew? Large and small stereotypes dissolved in the light of knowledge.

The more I dealt with these children, the more clearly I was able to see the mistakes I believed had been made in dealing with the Nazi past. One important mistake seemed to be the fact that Jews, understandably, had placed too much emphasis on their own fate. Thus the crimes of National Socialism against other minorities, against its own people and, ultimately, humanity, had been pushed into the background. Second, the Nazis had cleverly understood how to appeal to negative social emotions by implying that all Jews were rich Jews. Up until now the Jews had not done much to counteract this stereotype.

Even though I came from the shtetl and always carried this shtetl inside me, even though I dealt with different types of people in my daily work, the common Jewish people were overshadowed in my mind, too, by the great personalities of intellectual Vienna. Vienna seemed to me like an arcade, like a colonnade full of busts of great people. Not everyone knew that many of them were Jews. But with their questions and their ignorance, these schoolchildren made it clear to me that with this image of Jewish history and culture, an incorrect or at least skewed picture of Judaism had settled in their minds.

What was missing was a monument for the common Jews whose culture was the bedrock of great Jewish achievements. Vienna seemed like a particularly appropriate place to create a monument to the world of the shtetl. Particularly Vienna, because the sons and daughters of so many Jews from the East had given *fin-de-siècle* Vienna its character. Now people had come from the East again, as I mentioned earlier—and many resolved to stay and establish a new community. Yet Vienna was also a transit station, a geopolitical pivot point for Jews who came from the world of the East on their way to Israel or the West. Again, Vienna had become the dividing line between the old and the new worlds of Judaism.

It occurred to me that no one spoke about the little Jews. Jews and non-Jews were barely informed about those who really sustained this culture. Even less was known about the society that made this culture possible, or about those poor devils who created the society of the shtetl through the work of their hands and hearts. At most one had a literary, melancholy picture of them, no real understanding of lives. Yet who read the novels by Joseph Roth and Manès Sperber? Not the young students—the wider public that I was concerned about.

At the beginning of the eighties I thought about organizing an exhibition with the Jewish Welcome Service, and part of my motivation was to demonstrate the necessity for a Jewish museum in Vienna. On one of my trips to New York, through Peter Marboe, the director of the Austrian Cultural Institute in New York at that time, I met the journalist Joachim Riedl. He was enthusiastic about my idea and was instrumental in the realization of the exhibit as well as in editing the catalogue. His friend Peter Hoffman, who unfortunately died too young, organized a Jewish film week to accompany the exhibition.

There is a certain irony that my research for the exhibition, which we called "A Vanished World," first led me to Marboe. He was very interested in my idea and solidly supported my request. He referred me to the Bronfman Foundation for my research. They were said to have pictures, archival material, all the information that I would need for my exhibition. The irony of our encounter in New York was that later, in the era of Waldheim, Marboe was appointed head of the ÖVP. Thus Waldheim's later campaign director put me in contact with the World Jewish Congress (WJC).

At the World Jewish Congress I became acquainted with Israel Singer, Secretary General of the WJC, a man consumed with Jewish causes. He had taught political science and Near Eastern studies at universities in Israel and New York. In 1964 he was ordained a rabbi, and he likes to call himself a "rabbi without a pulpit." Both his parents came from Vienna and emigrated in 1938. Singer assured me that he would support my plan to organize this exhibition.

The World Jewish Congress, he told me openly, was interested in Vienna. At the time Israel had no diplomatic mission in the countries of the Eastern bloc. As the WJC needed a base from which to make contact with politicians in Austria and Eastern Europe, he was very interested in establishing communication with Poland, Hungary, Romania, and Czechoslovakia. I was proud to be able to work with him in making these contacts.

I arranged the connection between Kreisky's office and Israel Singer. Travel now flourished between Vienna and New York. I often picked up Singer from the airport, accompanied him to Kreisky, and met him again afterward. Singer always wears a yarmulke, the head covering that is considered a symbol of Jewish self-respect. Of course he also wore the yarmulke to his appointments with Kreisky, whereupon Kreisky remarked that the yarmulke reminded him of his grandparents. Singer and Kreisky discussed very practical issues concerning persecuted and repressed Jewish communities; they also spoke about the Talmud, about Jewish wisdom, in brief, about anything and everything. One day Singer left Kreisky's office at Ballhausplatz with a happy, even radiant smile. I asked him why. He said only: "That is one smart Jew!"

Austria's neutrality was just as helpful as Kreisky's reputation around the world. Sometimes, when it came to helping, one arrived at rather absurd combinations. One day Singer reported the tragedy of some Jewish girls who had been abducted from a ghetto in Syria and forced into brothels. On Kreisky's instructions the Austrian ambassador Herbert Amry obtained Cuba's assistance in getting the girls out of Syria and thus to safety.

In the eighties the main focus of the work of the World Jewish Congress was transferred to the East. Between 1968 and 1986, more than 260,000 Jews left the Soviet Union via Austria. Vienna was now an established political center. The Jews not only had nothing to fear here but could also benefit from its being a lively central point. Many interests coincided here. First was Kreisky's idea—one he had been proclaiming since the fifties—of making Vienna into a diplomatic meeting place primarily for security reasons and to create a safe zone in Central Europe radiating out of Austria. Then there were the interests of the WJC, to help the suppressed Jews in Eastern Europe and to intervene where Israel's hands were tied. And then there were my own dreams of making this city into a meeting place for Jewish people around the world. Now I had every reason for being satisfied with the role that Austria played.

Kreisky was, after all, a Jew at the head of the Austrian federal government. It was obvious that one would be proud of that. As with all great men, Kreisky was also a man of contradictions. The image of his relationship to Judaism, as well as the image of Kreisky as a self-hating Jew requires some correction. His aggressive criticism of Israeli Prime Minister Menachem Begin was purely politically motivated. Of course he should have been more moderate in his accusations against Begin, considering that in Austria it doesn't matter whether a Jew or a non-Jew says something against Jews: the applause always comes from the wrong side. Kreisky should have known that calling Begin "a political grocer . . . a little Polish lawyer or whatever he was from Warsaw . . . ." could only have the effect of being anti-Semitic here.

Incidentally, as it turned out, Kreisky's views about the peace process in the Near East were largely correct. I had mixed feelings, however, about some of his cabinet posts. His integration of old Nazis as ministers could still be taken as blunders. Perhaps I just lack a feeling for political realism. Kreisky's love affair with the FPÖ, the Austrian Freedom Party, under an SS man whose last name was Peter, I cannot remember his first, was much harder for me to accept—I thought it was outrageously schizophrenic. Nevertheless, pride and satisfaction at having a Jew as Austrian federal chancellor, something that Kreisky himself had believed to be impossible, outweighed everything else for me.

Naturally I was angry about his anti–Israel attitude. I couldn't understand why he would bow to the oil terrorists of OPEC, or how his interior minister Rösch could say goodbye to the terrorist leader Carlos at the airport with a handshake. At the same time, I have to admit that without Kreisky and Vienna it would have been impossible for almost a million people to have emigrated from the Soviet Union to Israel since 1948. It was also Kreisky who in 1967, as head of the Socialist Party, took part with Viennese socialists in a demonstration of support for an Israel threatened by the Six-Day War.

Kreisky was not a Zionist. He considered Begin a reactionary and was disappointed by his Socialist Party counterpart Shimon Peres, who he felt had not dealt with him sincerely. He complained about this to me more than once. It hurt him that the leaders of the Jewish State, who could have been his opposite numbers, did not have the stature of a man like Anwar Sadat. When one knew about Kreisky's personal relationship to Israel, one saw everything in a completely different light.

He felt that he had been deceived by Israeli politicians; he felt seriously insulted because they did not believe him that the peace process depended on introducing democracy to everyone who lived in Israel, including the Arabs.

Once I accompanied him, Heinz Fischer, and several others to a meeting of the Socialist International in Israel. When the children's choir sang *The Internationale* and then *Hatikvah*, the Israeli national anthem, Kreisky had tears in his eyes. He phoned me full of joy when his nephew from Israel came to visit, and he took him proudly to the May 1 celebrations. The young man was in the military at the time and wore his uniform, which made Kreisky even prouder. Although his nephew was only a normal draftee Kreisky introduced him everywhere as an officer.

Kreisky has a brother living in Israel who suffered since his childhood from mental illness. An attempt had been made to blame Kreisky for failing to take responsibility for him. It was said this brother lived like a beggar in Israel. I knew him and I knew that Kreisky sent him a respectable amount of money every month. On occasion Kreisky's mother also gave me money for him when I flew to Israel. As the relationship to his brother was so difficult and painful for him, Kreisky concentrated all his affection on his nephew.

Kreisky was a man whom one had to love and respect, not only because he left a considerable impression on world politics, but because he did not mince words. When he visited Washington I was convinced that the world press had never been so impressed by a politician from a small country as it was by Kreisky. What I respected was that in spite of all the demands, in spite of all criticism, he was always driven by love for a cause. Kreisky not only created the infrastructure for the transit of the Soviet Jews; he also respected their religious identity as Jews—although he was not religious—and arranged for prayer books to be sent to synagogues in the East.

• • •

All of this was carried out via Vienna. All of it made me proud. And none of it broke off when Kreisky resigned after the election of 1983. When Austrian Federal President Rudolf Kirchschläger visited America, accompanied by Foreign Minister Leopold Gratz, they met with leading representatives of Jewish life, among them numerous Austrian emigrants. Gratz, my old friend from the fifties, was greeted as an "especially welcome guest" by Rabbi Arthur Hertzberg, Vice President of the WJC. Relations between Austria and the WJC seemed to be running smoothly, so smoothly that I dared to make a request. I wanted the next congress of the WJC to be held in Vienna. I told Edgar Bronfman, President of the WJC, and Israel Singer how important it was to me to present Vienna as a city with normalized relations to Judaism. They understood what I had in mind. Bronfman said, "Yes, we want to help you."

In autumn 1984, the exhibition "A Vanished World" (The Lost World of Eastern European Jewry) was opened in Vienna by Federal President Rudolf Kirchschläger, accompanied by a week of Jewish films and an international symposium. Bronfman and Singer came to the opening and visited the exhibit. In one of the photographs Singer recognized his father as he was being forced by the Nazis to wash the street. This was wrenching, a dramatic moment. Nevertheless, I persuaded him not to make a public scandal out of his distress.

In the meantime, Helmut Zilk had become mayor of Vienna. One of his first acts was to invite New York Mayor Ed Koch to visit Vienna. Koch had expressed himself strongly about Austrian anti-Semitism. I helped to organize his trip, during which he visited the "Vanished World" exhibition and the "Documentation Archive of Austrian Resistance," and thus was able to form an impression of "another" Austria. Two years later, in 1986, he opened the acclaimed exhibition "Vienna 1900" in New York. This was another occasion to offer a different view of Austria abroad.

It was important to me not only to accompany internationally prominent personalities through the "Vanished World," but also to show it to schoolchildren and young people. I organized numerous tours, some for the Austrian armed forces. I can imagine that at least in some of those young heads some ideas were planted about who Jews are and what Jewish culture is; I hoped this exposure to the shtetl would show them it does not just consist of the representatives of high culture. Only ignorance creates the grounds for the prejudices and resentments to which the parents of these young people had fallen victim.

In January 1985 the international convention of the WJC did take place in Vienna. It was opened by Federal Chancellor Fred Sinowatz in the Hofburg Palace. Elie Wiesel, who won the Nobel Peace Prize the following year, gave the political address. I sat in the conference hall and saw one of the high points, one of the greatest days of my work in Vienna. The WJC had broken the spell, and although its mistrust of postwar Austria had not been entirely overcome, a first step had been taken. Six hundred Jewish delegates from all over the world had gathered in the building from whose balcony Hitler had greeted hundreds of thousands of enthusiastic Viennese in 1938.

At the same time Friedhelm Frischenschlager, the Minister of Defense, greeted a Nazi war criminal at the Graz airport with a delegation of the armed forces, and publicly shook his hand. It was Walter Reder, a former major in the Wehrmacht and SS officer. He had been serving time in Italian prisons since 1945 for the crime of having the entire town of Marzabotto near Bologna—1,830 people—wiped out in the last days of the war. A cry of public outrage swept through Austria. On the one hand, there was an outcry over the minister's gesture; on the other hand, the Freedom Party (FPÖ) defended him by saying that Reder had done his duty.

The atmosphere among the delegates of the World Jewish Congress, who had an underlying feeling of mistrust towards Austria anyway, turned to a mood of outrage. I sat there petrified. My dream disintegrated. Few of these delegates had wanted to come to Vienna in the first place. Israel Singer and a few other people had protested at first and then predicted that Vienna would never be accepted as a congress venue, because the Jews would never agree. Not until Foreign Minister Gratz had renewed my invitation officially in New York, not until Bronfman, Singer, and Koch had become acquainted with the Jewish community in Vienna through the "Vanished World" had they let themselves be persuaded to come to Vienna.

The congress, my congress was to be broken off. The delegates wanted to leave Vienna as quickly as possible. They began to pack their suitcases. One cannot forget that after 1945, the view of the WJC had been that no Jewish communities should or could be established in Austria or Germany. One cannot forget what the WJC had experienced with Austria in the matter of reparations. "Austria, that's a story all to itself . . . ." was the resigned statement of Nahum Goldmann, the longtime president of the WJC, who had been able to come to agreement with the German chancellor Adenauer about reparations, but not with Austria's representatives.

A disrupted congress would have been a catastrophe—for Austria, for Vienna, for me personally. I was torn. I abhorred what Frischenschlager had done, I shuddered at the thought that the FPÖ co-governed this country. Still Heinz Fischer and Ferdinand Lacina, the anti-Borodajkewicz demonstrators, were also members of this government as was my friend Leopold Gratz. There could be no doubts about the honorable motives of Fred Sinowatz. If the World Jewish Congress left now a wave of outrage would break loose in the world press that these men and Austria did not deserve.

I threw myself into the forefront of this conflict and in my distress asked Edgar Bronfman what to do. Bronfman was also in favor of leaving immediately, but explained to me that he was prepared to wait for a response from the Chancellor. Early on Sunday morning, I think it was seven-thirty, I called Sinowatz at home, informed him of the situation at the congress, and urgently asked him to talk with Bronfman to avert the worst.

Sinowatz called Bronfman at the Hilton Hotel immediately, apologized for Frischenschlager's behavior, and assured him that he too found the whole situation unpleasant and objectionable. At eight o'clock Bronfman summoned the delegates of the WJC to the foyer of the hotel and made a short speech. He essentially told them about his conversation: "Five minutes ago I spoke with Federal Chancellor Sinowatz, a very decent man. As long as people like Mr. Sinowatz have the say here, we will not leave. We will not break off our congress and leave in an uproar. We can't do that to the honorable people in this country. We're staying here." He reported in detail about what had been said between Sinowatz and himself. At the end, all of the delegates applauded. The crisis had been averted. The happiest person in that hotel foyer was this writer.

Once again I had been spared from inner conflict, once again I could direct my view forward. The disapproval of the events surrounding Reder's return was obviously shared by an overwhelming majority of the population. I continued to try to tell myself that the recurring signs of a repressed past were the problems of an older generation which would be settled with time. Even the 140,000 voters for neo-Nazi Norbert Burger in the presidential election of 1980, the numerous polls that confirmed the degree of latent anti-Semitism, and venomous expressions by the tabloid press seemed to me to be holdovers and isolated occurrences that didn't touch the anti-fascist and anti-racist consensus at the center of society.

From one year to the next this world of mine collapsed. I could see that this consensus was in danger. From the very center of society a stream of anti-Semitism burst forth, a stream whose undercurrent I had not wanted to acknowledge up until now. The break, out of which this stream rose to the surface, was called Waldheim.

I do not want to go to great lengths to explain the Waldheim affair. I have a different aim. I had built my life in this city. I had thought that this city was mature enough for its moral reincarnation. Waldheim showed me where I really lived. All the war criminals, the restitution refusers, the subtle and flagrant anti-Semites, the rabble-rousers from the tabloid press and the racists had not convinced me—Waldheim did. He forced me to confront my own illusions. He, who was the biggest repressor of all, showed me how much I myself had repressed in order to justify living in this country.

He was not a war criminal. But that was not the point. People who compared his case to François Mitterrand's, whose collaborator past had also been discovered, overlooked the fact that after the discovery Mitterand had taken an open position, without trying to deny what had happened. Waldheim, however, had withdrawn himself from the discussion. I could not excuse him for that. He was not capable of recognizing that the catastrophe of his discovered past represented a chance. Not the chance that he grasped, which was to get into office by mobilizing anti-Semitic resentment, but the chance, as a presidential candidate and possibly as president, to show this country how to cope with its past.

Instead of that he set about making it possible to arouse opinions against "certain circles," or at least to allow it. My own mental block loosened up during the Waldheim affair. For me, the question of whether or not he was a criminal was secondary; I had become inured to the idea of being able to encounter a Nazi criminal at any time, to be invited somewhere with one, to sit at the same table with one. After all, there were enough of them around. For me Waldheim did not represent a historic figure, but a figure of the present. While I felt sick when I saw the first photo of him in a Nazi uniform, it was not his behavior during Nazi times that was the problem, but rather his present behavior.

One of the many versions of the story of how the Waldheim affair came to light goes like this: In 1985, a reactionary officers' association had a commemorative plaque for Austrian Nazi General Alexander Löhr put up at the Vienna Stift Barracks. General Löhr was responsible for atrocities in the Balkans for which he was executed after 1945. One of the high-ranking officers closest to Löhr had been Kurt Waldheim, subsequently UN Secretary General and candidate for the office of Austrian Federal President. Thus the idea came up to investigate Waldheim's past. Bruno Kreisky, who heard the account from Israel Singer, describes this affair in his memoirs.

The indignation of the Western world directed itself against Waldheim because he took half the nation as hostage. "I'm being accused? Well then you are also being accused, and so is your father and your grandfather, because you were all soldiers," went his argument. And "all of us," according to Waldheim, "only did our duty." In Waldheim, Austria met itself—repressing the past, disregarding the truth, admitting nothing, dragging the matter out, perhaps not even being conscious of any guilt at all.

Everything that the country had tried to conceal was made visible through Waldheim. Waldheim could have done much to loosen the tension. But his opponents also made mistakes. Instead of leading a discussion about the role of the country, the attempt was made to seek proof for Waldheim's individual guilt. He, on the other hand, believed that with the evidence about his non-participation in killing, the correctness of his behavior was proven.

The SPÖ as well lacked the courage for a discussion of this nature. It was afraid of starting a civil war. Even then I believed—as I do now—this excuse vastly exaggerated. The Waldheim affair would have become a bitter confrontation no matter what. The older Jews had already begun to be afraid. The WJC felt that it had the moral right to agitate against Waldheim. I agreed with the WJC, but, on the other hand, I couldn't change the way I was. What was important to me was Vienna. Purposely I threw myself between the two sides to soften the attacks. Hadn't fifty-three percent of all the Viennese voted against Waldheim? I wrote a letter to Edgar Bronfman appealing to him on behalf of the decent people in this city to put an end to the campaign against Waldheim. The Jews here were going to have to live in fear again. Israel Singer, whose parents had been forced to leave Vienna in 1938, gave me an answer that was understandable from his point of view, but unbearable from mine: "If the Viennese Jews are afraid, they should leave."

In this situation it was good to have people like Leopold Gratz, who resigned as Foreign Minister because of Waldheim; and people like Helmut Zilk and Franz Vranitzky, who did their best to prevent the worst within Austria, and to make sure that my Jewish friends abroad did not get the impression that Waldheim *was* Austria. Moreover, a number of the ÖVP politicians were more than unhappy with Alois Mock's role as fanatic defender of Waldheim. I heard this from Stefan Koren as well as Erhard Busek, who had been vice-chancellor of Vienna.

Peter Marboe and Waldheim's press spokesman, Gerold Christian, were also some of the positive figures of these days, although politically they were on the other side. In the interest of the country I wanted to give Waldheim the chance to make some clarifying remarks before it was too late. I offered to mediate not because Christian and Marboe were positive personalities for me, but because I wanted to have my view of Austria back, my view of Vienna. During the climax of the crisis we met each other almost daily. I hit on the idea of arranging a talk between Waldheim and Ari Rath, who was then the editor-in-chief of the *Jerusalem Post* and who was coincidentally in Vienna at the time. Rath and Waldheim knew each other from the latter's term as UN Secretary General.

Ari Rath shared my opinion that for Waldheim the problem could be solved only by facing the nation and stating: "I witnessed this terrible time in our history. I saw no other way than to obey this regime. I saw many things and fully understood what kind of regime it was. I want to tell the youth of our country that we served a criminal regime."

Naturally, there never was an official meeting of Rath and Waldheim. There was an exceedingly bizarre scene. At a performance of the satiric sketch, "Herr Karl" by Qualtinger/Merz, I introduced Rath and Christian to each other. Subsequently Rath was supposed to meet with press-spokesman Christian alone. As he sat waiting in Christian's office in the Hofburg, a door opened discreetly and Waldheim stuck his head into the room. "Such a surprise, Mr. Rath is in Vienna!" And he drew him into his office for a chat, where he led the conversation into his problem. Ari Rath reported the same evening that Waldheim had promised to follow his advice. "I want to turn the clock back," he supposedly said. And Rath explained to him how it should be done.

Immediately I phoned Israel Singer and threatened him with all sorts of things, if Waldheim said these words the World Jewish Congress still did not stop their campaign. "I want this affair to end once and for all," I said and begged for restraint until Waldheim's televised speech, which was being anticipated with general suspense. The day after Waldheim's address, Singer phoned me and said: "You are a fool. That's how they are!" Waldheim's address did not contain a word of what he had promised Rath he would say.

Nor was Waldheim forthright with us, the well-meaning Jews. Although we were his political opponents, we were concerned about Austria and about our Jewish existence in Austria. Instead of speaking openly to break the spell of repression and possibly lead up to a clarifying discussion, he chose to equip Messrs. Mock, Holden, and Gruber with millions and send them around the world to create a more favorable climate for him. They returned with the idea that the Jews were against Waldheim only because they wanted reparations, or in other words, money.

Waldheim did not only allow all this to happen but encouraged it. He did nothing to avert talk about "certain circles," whereby the Jewish financial capital on the U.S. east coast was implied. He did not try to prevent the use of election slogans such as "We Austrians vote for whom we want" and "Now even more," which gave a strong signal for open anti-Semitism. In the daily newspaper *Die Presse* allusion was made to "international Jewry" and they wrote that "ominous business was being made from the past." Waldheim destroyed my world of the Heers, the Knolls, the Strassers, the Mlczochs, the Lunzers, and the Lacinas.

In spite of this I was able to prevent a court case that Waldheim had initiated against Bronfman. The date was tactfully set for Yom Kippur, the holiest day of the Jewish year. This provocation was not at all inopportune for Bronfman. He was all ready to charter a plane for his lawyers and staff to come to Vienna. That would have shown the Jewish world once again how insensitive Austria was, to have set this date, of all times, for the trial. It would have been a tragedy. Bronfman planned to review once more the Wehrmacht's role in the Holocaust, which could not have taken place without the material support of the Wehrmacht.

A terrible discussion would have broken loose in this country, which still insisted on the fact that its Wehrmacht soldiers had only done their duty. Then Austria was even less ready to have that discussion than it is today. I spoke with Franz Vranitzky about it, who agreed with my view that the trial should not take place. I gave him the idea of sending Bronfman a telegram for the Jewish New Year. Bronfman was impressed. He valued Vranitzky not only as a politician, but as a human being and as a man from the new Austria. I had already flown to London, to speak with Israel Singer once more, who was unrelenting towards Waldheim. Finally Gerold Christian succeeded in convincing Waldheim that it would be better to withdraw the suit.

I met Waldheim years later in May 1992 at the 150-year anniversary of the Vienna Philharmonic. He came toward me, bent over me, his nose hovering almost threateningly above me, took my hand, and didn't let go until we had been photographed. He said, "Dr. Zelman, I know what you have gone through. You're right, I must talk with you." After the first shock I looked him in the eyes. Then I understood that this old man had still not grasped what the whole thing was about. Nevertheless I had to answer him. "Dr. Waldheim, I cannot grant you absolution. You have to do that yourself. You must find the right way and the right words yourself!" Somehow I was sorry for him because he didn't have the courage, and because he still did not comprehend that the matter was not about my former suffering, but about his present deeds.

Yet, in a certain sense, he had defeated me, and *that* was something for which I could not forgive him. Against all the other challenges by Nazis, racists, and the like, I could have kept up my dreams and illusions. Not against Waldheim. However, it is obvious to me that distinct sides evolved, and that the indignation about what happened subsequently brought forth a wave of historical interest and commitment among the intellectuals and the young people. I only wished that this wave could have been mobilized through other channels.

As to the positive consequences of the Waldheim affair, one of them was Franz Vranitzky's declaration in parliament; he was the first Austrian head of state to speak about historic guilt on the part of Austria. I was able to assist from the sidelines, as I had a long conversation about this topic with my friend and former classmate Hugo Portisch before he drafted the declaration. In Vranitzky's cautious manner, it was included in a statement in parliament on the subject of Yugoslavia. Portisch and I had envisaged a special meeting of the parliament, at which representatives of all the countries involved in the war with Hitler-Germany were to take part.

I was completely satisfied with Vranitzky's declaration on his trip to Israel, which was also the first official visit to Israel by an Austrian chancellor. I felt very proud of this guiltless young man, as he was received by the Israel guard of honor. He represented my country in Israel in such a way that I didn't have to be ashamed. He did not try to camouflage Austria's past, he even put it in the foreground. That was impressive. All in all, I must say that Vranitzky steered Austria through the Waldheim affair with the greatest sense of decency possible.

I was also filled with pride when Teddy Kollek, mayor of Jerusalem, introduced the Austrian Minister of Education, Rudolf Scholten, as "the new face of Austria." Kollek was impressed by this intelligent, sensitive young Austrian, who he felt represented the new liberal leadership of the country.

In connection with Waldheim, I can't keep myself from divulging some of the side issues of this affair. I was angry with Simon Wiesenthal for keeping out of the matter for the longest time. He did it for obvious party considerations, in something that didn't allow party politics. Wiesenthal, who didn't hesitate to reproach Leopold Gratz for being a member of the Hitler Youth as a twelve-year-old, remained silent when it came to Waldheim. Wiesenthal knew that Waldheim had not been a war criminal, but Waldheim lied when he claimed not to have seen or heard anything. In Salonika the whole marketplace was full of Jews for days before they were transported to Auschwitz. Everyone could see how these people were crowded together in the churches. Waldheim was stationed three miles away but claimed he did not know that Jewish transports were taking place.

Wiesenthal did not say a word against Mock when he pointed to "certain circles." On the contrary, he met Mock almost daily at a coffeehouse to give him advice. I wanted him to say something like: "Gentlemen, this can't go on. This is not how to solve the problem. A discussion should take place here, but instead you are stirring up anti-Semitism! Stop it! And you, Dr. Waldheim, own up to what you have seen!" I waited in vain for such words, but he was silent concerning Mock, and he did not speak to Waldheim until much later and then only under American pressure.

Mock himself had put his whole foreign ministry to work on this affair, not to initiate an open discussion, but to prevent such a discussion. In any case, the foreign minister of this country did not represent the interests of the Jews of this country. He wasn't concerned about the conflict with the truth; he was concerned about keeping up the image.

During these months, unbelievable things occurred. Someone proposed to me that each Jew should contribute one thousand shillings to protect the Jews. Since there were fifty thousand Jews in Vienna (in truth there are far fewer!), this would certainly amount to a large sum. I stood up and called him a swine. "Do you think we are still in the Middle Ages, when the Jews had to pay tribute to save themselves?" I asked indignantly, so that the people in the coffeehouse turned around surprised.

Even Jews became infected and tried to hush things up. Peter Landesmann, who identified himself as "an active member of the Jewish community," wrote a curious article in *Die Presse* on the subject of anti-Semitism. He remarked that Edgar Bronfman was a "co-owner of an internationally important company that manufactured alcoholic drinks," while the World Jewish Congress was a small office "with approximately thirty employees" which due to its "unimportance" did not even run the risk of breaking up. It bothered me that the racist reproach that Bronfman was only a "whisky dealer" was repeated from the Jewish side.

As far as the World Jewish Congress was concerned, this organization was generally portrayed in Austria as a bunch of misguided fanatics. The Jews know exactly what the WJC is. It is a voluntary, loose association of Jewish communities and organizations all over the world. Founded in 1936, it intervened wherever it could during times of Jewish persecution, founded aid committees, sought possibilities for immigration and emigration. What is striking for Austria is that in 1938, only Mexico and the WJC protested to the Third Reich against the *Anschluss* of Austria.

After 1945 the WJC organized aid activities and assisted in the prosecution of war criminals. Later the President of the WJC, Nahum Goldmann, negotiated the question of reparations with Konrad Adenauer and, with less success, with the Austrian government. The WJC is one of the sponsors of Yad Vashem in Israel, cares for oppressed Jews in the East and in Arab countries, and fights against anti-Semitism and racism. Only in Austria could it happen that this organization could be portrayed as the spiteful, self-important creation of a whisky dealer, and that not only by tabloid anti-Semites but by an "active member of the Jewish community."

It seems as though many people were interested in preventing this country from looking in the mirror after fifty years, and furthermore, were ready to call those who demanded it nest foulers and bad Jews. Mock was even prepared to pay money to a group of anti-Zionist Jews in America only to show that there were also good Jews, who weren't interested in a confrontation with Waldheim. From one day to the next, I now lived in a world full of dirty little conflict winners who all had honest faces. And I lived in a world in which the political right was reforming and suddenly dared to come forward with revisionist provocations. "He who sows Waldheim will reap Haider," someone accurately stated at the climax of the Waldheim crisis. In fact, the revisionist connection had never broken off since 1945. The openness with which someone like Jörg Haider makes his provocations when he speaks of the "orderly employment policy in the Third Reich," or calls concentration camps "detention camps" thus denying millions of murders, is part of a phenomenon that has become socially acceptable again and shows me where I live.

After Waldheim I was in shock. I still saw what was positive, however, and took up the fight again. The outcry of the intellectuals, the indignation of the youth, the steadfastness of many politicians comforted me. I took up my work again, conscious that as part of this city I was being used and taken advantage of. I flew to America and declared that Vienna was not anti-Semitic; fifty-three percent of the Viennese population had voted against Waldheim.

Meanwhile I reproached myself for making these concessions for the sake of public relations. On the other hand, my ulterior motive was still valid: If I let myself be used, I wanted to get something in return. Yet I was often ashamed that I let the others believe that they had used me, when in truth I had used them. I tried not to make any compromises, although I always ended up making them after all. I always wanted to live according to certain principles and yet I couldn't always do it.

After Waldheim it was plainer to me than ever that the focal point of my work had to be with those who were born after 1945. The project "Welcome to Vienna, the City of Your Grandparents" was planned for the commemorative year 1988 (fifty years after the *Anschluss*). The idea was to invite the grandchildren of Jews who had been forced to leave in 1938 as guests of non-Jewish Viennese families. The journalist Susi Schneider organized a series of "Jewish Heritage" exhibitions in New York, Miami, Los Angeles, and Chicago. Peter Marboe, former vice-chancellor Erhard Busek, and a prominent professor, Anton Pelinka, spoke at the openings. There was great interest on the part of young people.

The grandparents objected. "Absolutely not," many of them said. "We will not send our grandchildren to Vienna, when no one ever made the effort to apologize to us or show any concern for us." Then I had the idea of first inviting the elderly and exiled Viennese Jews to come back. The children were allowed to come only with their consent. Afterward their grandparents sent me thank you letters. Many of them said: "Dr. Zelman, you are a wise man. One has to begin the way you did." Others told me that what I was doing was great, but had I been in Vienna in 1938, I wouldn't be able to do it.

It was astonishing for me that when these older people came, they didn't waste a single word about reparations or restitution. There were over four hundred young people whom I invited in 1988, and over twelve hundred old people whom I could invite to Vienna in the following years. For this purpose I demanded and received from Zilk and Vranitzky the money budgeted for the conference of the American Jewish Committee which had been cancelled. The older people were touched by this gesture. As it turned out, what embittered them the most was that since 1945, they had heard nothing, not a word from either Vienna or Austria.

I have concentrated my adult life on showing the world that a cosmopolitan atmosphere can exist in Vienna again, which includes the capacity for a thriving Jewish community. When I accompany the old Viennese to the synagogue, when they meet the rabbi, many of them cry because they still recognize this place. Some of them want to go see their old apartments, just to see them once more. Some of them ask for a room with a view of a certain park.

When it's possible, I fulfill all of these wishes. One lady wrote that she wanted to stay at the Imperial Hotel. I thought she was being presumptuous until I found out more about her. She had lived on Dumbastrasse at the time that Hitler came to Vienna and took a suite at that hotel. Since her apartment faced the Imperial, she was put under house arrest and her windows were darkened. She was embarrassed in front of her Christian girlfriends, who had all hurried to the Ringstrasse to watch. Now this disgrace was to be righted. Of course she got her room in the Imperial.

Another time there was a reception in City Hall at which Zilk and Vranitzky were expected to appear. A lady sat on a bench in the park of City Hall. I went to look for her and saw her sitting there with a peaceful smile on her face. I asked her why she didn't come to dinner. She answered that she was simply enjoying sitting here on this park bench in Vienna and not being chased away because she was a Jew.

It was important to me to bring the ordinary people back to Vienna, those who perhaps didn't have the money for such a trip. One of them had been the only Jewish railroad engineer of the Austrian railway. Another had no interest in museums, or in the Hotel Sacher; he only wanted to go home to the Floridsdorf district. He was a true proletarian. Once on the other side of the bridge, he took a wide-legged stance, tore open his sports jacket, beat his breast, and yelled with the broadest Floridsdorf accent: "Here I am!"

The first twenty children who had come here long before "Welcome to Vienna" were students I had spontaneously invited to Vienna at a meeting in New York. They called themselves the "Zelman Kids"; they are grown-up now and doing various things—professors, doctors—we still keep in touch. They gave me a heavy silver pencil. I gave this pencil to Helmut Zilk when he awarded me the Gold Honorary Medal of the City of Vienna.

I think very highly of Helmut Zilk. He has visions and emotions and I have seen him rage, laugh, and cry. I am convinced that politics should be made not only by dry realists. I always got along better with emotional people as partners. One had to understand Zilk's habit of exploding when he wasn't satisfied with something. Soon afterward he would be in a good mood again. When the conductor Lorin Maazel spoke critically about Vienna, Zilk raged. "Why? Why?" he asked me, as if *I* had spoken critically. I answered, "Helmut, he was wronged." He considered briefly. Perhaps he secretly thought I was right. But he never expressed it. He is a man who likes to have the last word.

Teddy Kollek, the legendary mayor of Jerusalem, came from Vienna. He often said that he would not go back to Austria. Zilk insisted upon it. He stubbornly refused to accept Kollek's refusal. He wanted Kollek to visit. So I made my way to Jerusalem and said to Teddy Kollek: "Before you stands a boy who was in a concentration camp, who has been given a lot by Vienna. For him Vienna is the city that he fought for in his fight against Hitler. Hitler wanted to destroy it, but today a thriving Jewish community exists in Vienna. Zilk is mayor of this city. He means it sincerely. Please come!"

Kollek looked at me and said, "What a big heart you have! I will think about it."

I did that for Zilk because I was convinced that he was serious. Also Kollek is an important person for me. His dream concerned a free, peaceful Jerusalem, in which everyone would have his place. Kollek actually did consider it, and his visit to Vienna was a huge success. In Los Angeles Kollek visited the exhibition "Jewish Heritage and Mission." That was the breakthrough in our relationship. The great old man visited my exhibit accompanied by Erhard Busek, vice-chancellor at the time. They filled me with pride.

I began to get young Austrians to talk with Kollek in Jerusalem. Kollek was deeply frustrated that the Austrians did so little for their relationship to Israel, as opposed to the Germans, yet his frustration decreased through these talks. When he finally met Zilk in Jerusalem, I felt with great satisfaction that both of them communicated on the same wavelength. I saw them sitting on a stone bench above the panorama of Jerusalem, talking with one another. My two mayors: Kollek, mayor of my heart, and Zilk, the mayor of my city.

Zilk had a problem: his impatience. He wanted a quick reconciliation. When the ORF (Austrian Radio and Television) made a documentary about Vienna-Jerusalem, which had been my idea, a few people appeared in it who said they would never come back, they never wanted to see Vienna again. Zilk was furious, called me up and shouted into the telephone: "How can these people say something like this, after all we've done!"

I always tried to explain to him that it will take generations to compensate for the years from 1938 to 1945 and the years thereafter, as well. For decades Austria did nothing to bring about a reconciliation. How could Zilk believe that after only five years of work he could enjoy the fruits of this reconciliation? For decades the Austrians had not deigned to give these people a word—I don't even want to speak about restitution. Not once had anyone said: "Come back, you are our citizens!" Zilk had difficulty comprehending that. He could not understand that it was not his good offices that were being denied, but that these efforts were weighed against the history of the Second Republic. Fifty years without love, without a hand being extended. The Republic had been blinded after 1945. These gestures wouldn't have cost it anything because, after all they had experienced, the exiled Jews wouldn't have come back anyway. It wouldn't have had anything to do with money, just with a gesture.

Zilk had motivated me with his ideas; he also let himself be motivated by mine. In association with his advisor Kurt Scholz, the thinker in the background, and his Vienna cultural counselor Ursula Pasterk, he did more for the Jews in this city than almost any politician. The Jewish Museum, Jewish schools, the memorial against war and fascism, go back to Zilk and his team. Even the place of my daughter's wedding was his idea. For the first time in the history of the Vienna City Hall a Jewish wedding was held there. Zilk welcomed it as a way of showing how integrated the Jewish community had become in his city.

But then he would fly into one of his well-known rages when he heard that a Jew in New York had published an article criticizing Vienna. He couldn't get over the fact that no matter how impressive his achievements were, they couldn't wash away history. When he yelled about something on the telephone, I would point out to him that the Spanish Jews did not forgive Spain until five hundred years after the expulsion. Since Vranitzky's apology, however, just a few years have gone by!

A few years ago, I drove to Ebensee in a limousine with Scholten, the Minister of Education. It was summertime. The limousine glided down the same village road that we had stumbled along daily as prisoners on our way to the mine shaft. The sun was shining, the balconies were bursting with begonias. It was a peaceful scene. It seemed as though nothing else could ever have happened there than a chain of boring, sunny summer days filled with flowers. For one terrible minute I asked myself if I had only dreamed everything. The past was back again. The car turned the corner. The minute was over. I forced myself to return to the present.

I was a child until I ended up in Vienna. From that moment on I had to be a man. A man who had missed having a youth. But there is one thing I never gave up, despite or perhaps because of my lost youth: dreaming. My greatest dream was to make the city in which I had landed, the city that the so-called Führer wanted to make free of Jews, my city.

In Vienna I found people who reached out to me and helped me with my plans. I also helped them with theirs. And if they believe that they used me, they can believe it. But I didn't do it for them. I was easy to use, but for my own dream. That others profited by using me, the city of Vienna, the Republic of Austria, that I am happy to admit.

But when it comes down to it I did it for myself. I won my fight against Hitler because against all hopes there is a lively Jewish community again, because he did not succeed in making the city free of Jews. And I won because I succeeded in living my life after survival.

EPILOGUE

*L*ife after survival once in a while brings forth the most beautiful and wonderful experiences but the saddest and most absurd stories as well. I want to tell two of them.

The first takes place in Florida, in 1993, on a ship where Holocaust survivors are meeting. The guests are brought to an island by boat. I notice a woman who draws attention to herself through her loud and exaggerated behavior. She asks everyone where they come from, and asks me as well. From Vienna, is my answer.

In the evening I see her again, very elegantly dressed. We get to talking again. It turns out that she was in Bad Ischl and Bad Goisern as a DP. Was I, too? Yes, I was! Whom does she remember? Not many people. But there were two bright boys from Poland, dreamer types, named Leon and Rysiek, whom she remembers well. Did I know them? "Yes," I said, "And how! One of the two is standing before you!" She cried out with joy and ran around the restaurant, telling everyone the story about Leon who had turned up again. The gathering talked about nothing else the entire evening.

A second story: A trip to a conference in New York. I arrive at Kennedy Airport. At customs a man sees my Austrian passport, looks up something on the computer, takes me aside and leads me into a side room. Two people are sitting there.

The man says: "You have to wait here."

I say: "I have to go to my conference."

"Anyone can say that. Where were you in the German army?"

"What do you mean army? I was in a concentration camp!"

An officer sitting there hears that. "Where were you born? In Poland? Write down your name and address!"

"Fellows, are you crazy?" The Austrian consul is waiting outside!" Gradually I am getting nervous.

A female officer appears with "Rosenblum" on her badge. I rise politely.

"Sit down!" she says.

"Mrs. Rosenblum, I am a Jew, just like you!"

"Then what are you doing here?"

"I don't know."

After three hours of waiting I am taken by taxi to the hotel. The consul left ages ago. I called my friends from the WJC; it was already one o'clock in the morning. I wanted to know what happened. They promised me to put me in touch with someone responsible in Washington the next day.

The next day I called Washington. The person responsible was none other than Neil Sher, the "Waldheim Watchlist man" head of the Office of Investigation at the Department of Justice. When he heard what had happened to me, he got behind it, and found out the following: Due to the watchlist all Austrians and Germans who were denied entry into the United States are listed in the computer. My name also appeared on the list because, at the time, all of those who did not get a visa due to health reasons were also put on the list.

The Department of Justice wrote me a letter of apology. The next day Mrs. Rosenblum came by. She also apologized and explained she had only been doing her job, as my name was on the list. Then she cried in shame for having done that to me. I comforted her. After all, everyone entering the country is checked. They are looking for Nazis. And due to my case the lists were corrected. Anyone who was once denied entry for health reasons is now spared these difficulties.

I suppose I should also mention the fine honors that were conferred on me. There was no lack of these kinds of things: prizes, medals, and all kinds of praise which made me very happy and filled me with enormous pride. I also had the honor of meeting President Bill Clinton.

I especially want to mention two honors I received in Vienna. In 1992 I was awarded the Renner Prize. I was happy that I could dedicate half of the money to the Roma and Sinti as a symbol that the Nazis' extermination machine did not affect only the Jews, but other minorities as well. The honor I value most took place on the occasion of my being named "Professor." I requested the then-Minister of Education to make an exception and hold the ceremony outside of the ministry. "We don't hold private ceremonies," I was informed. Nevertheless, in my case the minister was ready to make an exception.

The ceremony took place in the freshly renovated ceremonial rooms of the Jewish Community of Vienna on Seitenstettengasse, at the place where everything had begun for us as students in 1947. Near this site, Eichmann had calculated and speculated. Erika Weinzierl, professor of history, delivered the speech; she had to stop a number of times because she was choked with emotion. Now widely renowned, Weinzierl was one of the first contributors to the *Echo*. For me she represents the epitome of a forthright and sincere Austria. Everyone was there, not just the prominent politicians, but also the old Jews who had invited us to *shabbes* dinner and then stuck a piece of cake into our pockets, and old friends such as Dr. Mlczoch. It was snowing, yet there were people standing all the way out to the street. "Here is where my dream began in Vienna," I said in my acceptance speech.

All of these honors would have meant nothing if politicians like Zilk, like Vranitzky, like Scholten, and many others had not made my activities possible in the first place. If it hadn't been for them, my dreams would have never materialized. I served them well, closing my eyes and ears to some things, only to finally hear the long-awaited speech that Vranitzky delivered in Israel, or to get the money to send invitations to hundreds of exiled Jews, or to see a school emerge in Jerusalem, renovated with means provided by the Austrian federal government.

In that school, the Rehavia High School, there is a multi-purpose hall that was not financed with public money but with private donations and with the other half of my Renner Prize money. The donations primarily came from schoolchildren, from young Austrians. This hall serves as a meeting place and place of reconciliation with young Israelis. In 1995, to celebrate the fiftieth anniversary of Nazi Germany's capitulation, this hall opened with a gathering for young Jews, Muslims, and Christians, five hundred of them from Austria.

It was named the Leon Zelman Hall. A sixty-seven-year-old man stood there, crying for joy, because he is an emotional person. At night he tells his mother how wonderful it was and that now things are good. Not everything, but a great part of life is, after survival.